THE DO-IT-YOURSE

ESCAPE ROOM

BOOK

THE DO-IT-YOURSELF ESCAPE ROOM BOOK

A PRACTICAL GUIDE TO WRITING YOUR OWN CLUES, DESIGNING PUZZLES, AND CREATING YOUR OWN CHALLENGES

PAIGE ELLSWORTH LYMAN

Skyhorse Publishing

Skyhorse Publishing books may be purchased in bulk at special discounts for sales promotion, corporate gifts, fund-raising, or educational purposes. Special editions can also be created to specifications. For details, contact the Special Sales Department, Skyhorse Publishing, 307 West 36th Street, 11th Floor, New York, NY 10018 or info@skyhorsepublishing.com.

Skyhorse® and Skyhorse Publishing® are registered trademarks of Skyhorse Publishing, Inc.®, a Delaware corporation.

Visit our website at www.skyhorsepublishing.com.

10 9 8 7 6 5 4

Library of Congress Cataloging-in-Publication Data is available on file.

Cover design by Mona Lin

All photographs were shot and edited by Joshua Lyman, except for the author's portrait, which was shot by Melanie Ellsworth.

Print ISBN: 978-1-5107-5880-3
Ebook ISBN: 978-1-5107-5881-0

Printed in China

*To my mom, for encouraging me to write escape rooms,
and to her mom, for encouraging me to write*

Contents

Introduction

You're in a room. The door is locked. Around you are locked chests, mysterious paintings, suspicious mementos, and messages in code. The secret to unlocking the door and escaping must be in this room somewhere. You just have to find it first. . . . Are you in a spy movie? No! You're in an escape room.

An escape room is a type of game or challenge that's increasing in popularity around the world. In an escape room, players are locked in a room and have to search for clues, work together, and solve puzzles to escape, usually before a set timer expires. Escape rooms are fun because they make players feel like they really are in a tense or exciting situation, where the stakes are high and time is of the essence. The final escape is so rewarding.

There are commercial escape rooms in lots of cities. In these establishments, you pay money (often around twenty to thirty dollars a person) to enter a room and play through the challenges. It can be a lot of fun! However, commercial escape rooms might not be feasible for all groups and occasions. They are expensive, and sometimes if you have a large group, there might be too many people to fit in one facility at a time.

There are also play-at-home escape room options, like boxed games or downloadable kits. These challenges can be fun, but they're not quite the same as authentic escape rooms, often missing key elements like physical props, searching for and finding clues, or activities that manipulate objects in fun ways.

The good news is that there's another option! With some work and creativity, you can create your own real-life escape room in any room you choose.

DIY escape rooms usually have a host or game master. The host stays in the room with the players, oversees the game, and offers hints if the players get stuck. Depending on how the game is structured, a host might interact with the players even more than that. You as the game creator will most likely play the role of the host.

When you host your own escape room, you won't be able to play with your guests. You'll know all the secrets and answers as you write them. However, watching others play through a room you've created can be just as rewarding as playing one yourself.

A DIY escape room in a bedroom in a home, made with furniture and props from other rooms in the house, decorations found at a thrift store, and temporary wallpaper.

Why escape rooms?

- They're good team-building opportunities.
- They can break the ice and bring people together.
- They require critical thinking, observation, and communication.
- They're fun!

Why DIY escape rooms?

- They're customizable to your players in difficulty, theme, and style of puzzles.
- They're less expensive.
- They're fun to make.
- They're just as fun to play!

It is true that a DIY escape room most likely won't feel as professional as a commercial one. However, the goals of commercial escape rooms and DIY escape rooms are different. Commercial escape rooms have the goal of making money (and have money to spend to make that happen). The purpose of a do-it-yourself escape room is to have fun and meet a specific need of a specific group of people (and the room has the flexibility to make that happen).

Even when your props and puzzles are homemade, a great theme, plot, and structure will help imaginative players have just as much fun in a DIY escape room as a commercial one.

I still love and frequently play commercial escape rooms. They're great for lots of occasions, but not all. Creating your own escape room might be just what you need, and this book will tell you everything you need to know to do it!

This book is divided into two parts. Part one talks about the larger aspects of creating an escape room: theme, plot, room selection, difficulty, and running the event. Part two goes through clue and puzzle types, offering eight categories of puzzles and hundreds of ideas and examples.

Creating a whole escape room is a challenge, but a fun one! Let's get started!

Part 1
Room Creation

① Theme and Narrative

The most basic escape room is a collection of clues, puzzles, and tasks in a room that all ultimately lead to a final goal, like getting past one locked door. Here's a representation of a basic room like this, a structure we can grow on later:

Basic Escape Room

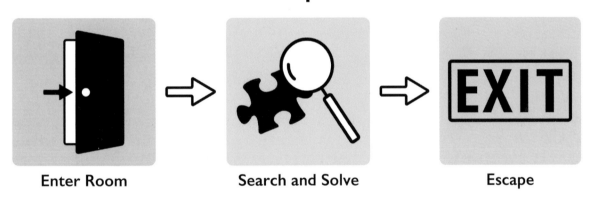

Enter Room   **Search and Solve**   **Escape**

People would likely find even this simple challenge engaging. However, there are things escape room creators can do to make escape rooms even more immersive and fun.

Escape Room Themes

One thing that can add an element of fun to a room is a theme. A theme ties the puzzles and decorations in an escape room together. The theme might be historical (Victorian England), fictional (castles and dragons), or inspired by a movie (spies and espionage). If the theme is Victorian England, the decorations should reflect that: dark colors, padded chairs, ornate swirls. So should the puzzles: perhaps messages hidden in paintings or coded in handwritten letters. A Victorian themed room should not, for example, use invisible ink and a black light. A black light *would* be a great clue type for a spy-themed room.

Here's a representation of a simple themed escape room:

Themed Escape Room

Enter Room   Decorations, Puzzles, and Clues Fit a Theme   Escape

When you write your escape room, get creative and choose a theme! To get you started, here are some ideas.

Theme Ideas

- **Any Modern Decade**—Twenties, fifties, seventies, eighties
- **Historic Periods**—Victorian England, the Old American West, Ancient Egypt, Ancient Greece, ancient civilizations of the Americas, the Titanic, pirates, World War II, any specific time and place in history
- **Places**—Library, hotel, submarine, power plant, apartment, office, school, airport, train station, cave, castle, playground, art museum, history museum, bank, train, cabin, mansion, theater, locker room, stadium, church, boat, prison, bar, island, tomb
- **Professions**—Archaeologist, jungle explorer, secret agent, detective, assassin, burglar, inventor
- **Subjects**—Art, science, math, music, literature
- **Science Fiction**—Spaceships, secret labs, time travel, aliens, superheroes, the apocalypse, other planets

- **Science Fact**—Space stations, research, nuclear facility, disease control labs
- **Fantasy**—Castles, dragons, wizards, steampunk, Atlantis
- **Paranormal**—Ghosts, werewolves, vampires, magicians
- **Horror**—Zombies, serial psycho killers, medical experimentation, mummies, monsters, morgues, anywhere haunted
- **Animals**—Zoos, dinosaurs, mythical creatures, pet stores
- **Seasons**—Christmas, Halloween, Easter
- **Factories**—Toys, candy, sweets, furniture, clocks, anything
- **Military**—Bunkers, coast guard, aircraft carrier, missile facility
- Any movie, video game, or book

Your decorations, if you're doing them, should fit into your theme. As DIY escape room creators, unlike commercial escape room creators, we're often limited by budget and space. This means our sets and decorations usually aren't as elaborate. Even if your whole room isn't decked out, you can do your best to remove items that don't fit your pirate theme (like a computer) and bring in decorations that do (like crates or wooden furniture). Then we'll ask our players to use their imaginations, which is A-OK. Every escape room, even a commercial one and especially a DIY one, requires imagination.

TIP:
If you're drawing from history, try customizing your theme to your own city or town. My family has attended a favorite summer ranch for years, and once I planned an escape room to play there that incorporated the history of the ranch, including a rich oil baron and a buried treasure (I'll admit it was fictionalized a little). Unless your goal is to provide an accurate historical lesson, there's no rule against embellishing to make it more exciting.

In addition to decorations, your clue and puzzle types should also fit your theme. If you're doing a historic theme, don't use technology that wasn't around at the time. If your theme is ancient Egypt, code your messages in hieroglyphics instead of Morse code.

Even though, as DIYers, we often don't have the budget and space commercial escape rooms have to work with, there are also some limitations we don't have to live by. One is copyright. If you are charging money for your escape room, you can't advertise it as taking place in a specific castle from a famous book/movie franchise. For your own escape room in your own home, you're free to recreate any room in Hogwarts you want. Just don't charge for it!

Also, in choosing decorations and props, we don't necessarily have to worry about choosing items that are extra durable. A commercial escape room could have dozens of unrelated people searching, touching, and using the props in a room in a single day. That might not be a challenge you'll have to face, if, for example, your escape room is in your own home with people you personally know and will be played only once or a few times. If you decide to create an ocean-themed escape room in your house and want to incorporate a more fragile decoration like a fish tank, you are much freer to do that than a commercial escape room would be.

A collection of escape room puzzles and props on a cowboy theme.

Several things can guide you in choosing a theme. You might choose one based on the room you have to work with. If you are hosting the escape room at your workplace, maybe your theme can be a haunted office building. Your players can also help guide your theme. If the escape room is for your twelve-year-old son and his friends, you'll probably want a theme suited to him, like his favorite book. Your theme can also be guided by your plot or narrative, which we'll get into next, and the types of puzzles and clues you'll want to use, which will be covered in part two.

Escape Room Narratives or Plots

I mentioned escape rooms that have no theme (just a chain of puzzles). We've also talked about escape rooms that do have a theme (cohesive decorations and puzzle types). Escape rooms can take it a step further by having a plot or narrative.

In these escape rooms, there's an explanation for why the players are trapped in the room and what they need to do to escape, as well as possible answers to a few other questions.

Questions Answered by an Escape Room Plot

- Why are the players in the room?
- How did they get there?
- What do the players need to do to escape or succeed?
- What's at stake if they don't escape?
- Why do they need to hurry? (Most escape rooms have a time limit and need to generate a sense of urgency.)
- Who is the host, why is he or she there, and why is he or she giving hints? (*Optional*: You might want to create a room where you pretend there is no host, even though you will probably want someone there to give hints.)

A narrative doesn't have to answer all of these questions. At the minimum, it should explain why the players are in the room and what they need to do to win or escape.

Narratives can be set up before the game starts, usually by the host reading or explaining something to the players or possibly playing an audio recording or a video. The narrative can even be unfolded bit by bit as players find and read things within the room.

Often escape room narratives are "bookend" narratives, with most of the important story information communicated at the beginning and end of the game.

Escape Room with a Bookend Narrative

Enter Room — An evil wizard locked you in his lair — Clues on Theme but Separate from Narrative — Escape before he comes back and turns you all into toads — EXIT — Escape

Escape room narratives can be tricky to come up with, especially when you're trying to balance the amount of information or backstory needed. You don't want to bog your players down with too many details at the beginning when they're mostly just excited to play. A good narrative, however, can make your players feel more invested.

Narratives can actually go a step further and answer one more question: Why are all these puzzles and clues in the room? Many escape rooms have a fun theme and a narrative that bookends the room (how players got there and what happens when they escape), but the puzzles and clues in the room are mostly left unexplained. Your players are trapped in an enemy spy's hideout? Then why did the spy leave a series of clues that ultimately lead your players to escape?

Instead, an escape room can have a plot with puzzles and clues that actually tie into the narrative. Building on our wizard example:

Escape Room with a Full Narrative

Enter Room

An evil wizard locked you in his lair. Complete his spell book and work the right incantations to escape the room before he comes back and turns you all into toads.

Narrative Explains/Incorporates Puzzles and Clues

Escape

The boundary between a bookend narrative and a full narrative can be a fuzzy one. Think of it as more of an escape room narrative continuum. Maybe you don't have a narrative. Maybe you have a leak-proof plot that ties everything together. Most likely, you're somewhere in between.

No one type of escape room is the right one. Yours will depend on your players and your goals. In the end, it's really about helping your players have a fun team-building experience, which doesn't need to require a perfect plot.

Narrative Examples

Since we've talked about theme ideas, let's talk about narrative ideas, too. Even though we're talking about escape rooms, the goal doesn't just have to be to escape. In his paper "The State of Escape: Escape Room Design and Facilities," Scott Nicholson includes the results of a survey of 175 commercial escape room companies around the world. Their goals were much more varied than just escape.

Escape Room Goals (from Scott Nicholson's paper "The State of Escape")[1]

- Escape a specific unpleasant place
- Investigate a crime or mystery
- Engage with the supernatural
- Solve the murder
- Defuse the explosive device
- Be an adventurer
- Gather intelligence or espionage
- Carry out a heist
- Find the missing person
- Help create something (such as a cure, a potion, etc.)
- Military operations
- Free another person or animal
- Survive!
- Carry out an assassination

As you can see, escape rooms don't just have to be about escape, even if that is the ultimate goal. Working in another goal can add to the narrative, make an escape room plot more unique and exciting, and give you more material to work with when you add clues and puzzles.

Looking at the list above can help you come up with some narratives, especially when you combine it with the list of themes. Here are some more examples of escape room narratives. (Feel free to use any of them!)

---

1 Nicholson, "The State of Escape," 7.

Broad Narratives

- Someone Kind (a rich relative with a will, a billionaire, a factory owner) locked you in a room with a test of wits. If you can escape, you'll get Something Good (lots of money, a mansion, a chocolate factory).
- Someone Friendly (a boss, a mentor, a magician) needs your help to do Something Important (find some lost information, search for clues, find the real murderer) to help him or her out.
- Something Bad (space pirate attack, computer failure, natural disaster, zombie apocalypse) happened. You need to do Something Important (reprogram the computer, communicate with someone on the outside, turn on the power) to fix it and escape.
- Someone Evil (a psychopath, aliens performing human experimentation, a murderer) locked you in a room and set up a test of wits. If you can escape, you won't be killed.
- Someone Nefarious (a science corporation, a corrupt government, a wizard) locked you in a room. Luckily, Someone Friendly (a team member, a previous inmate, the wizard's good apprentice) left a series of hidden clues that will help you escape.
- Someone Villainous (a spy, a thief) did Something Bad (sabotaged a submarine, infiltrated a factory, stole something) that left you trapped. You need to figure out what he or she did and fix it (stop the leak, diffuse the bomb, return the stolen goods) to escape and survive.

Specific Narratives

- You are explorers who have discovered an ancient Egyptian tomb. After you enter, the tomb seals shut and you find you are trapped. You have to search and solve to get past the puzzles and booby traps so you can escape the curse of the pharaoh and live.
- You are private investigators on a case, trying to catch a famous art thief. You are in the hotel room he just stayed in while he robbed a museum. You have to follow the clues left behind to figure out what he stole and where he fled so the authorities can catch him.
- You are art thieves in a museum, trying to steal a famous work of art stored in the curator's office. You have to get past the curator's quirky security measures by searching and solving to make it out with the painting before the security guards are alerted to your presence and arrest you.
- On a dare, you enter a vacant house in your town. After you enter, the door locks and you realize that the rumor that it's haunted must be true. You have to search and solve the puzzles set up by the ghosts if you want to escape.
- You have been captured by a corrupt government and thrown into a prison cell. A previous inmate left some clues and puzzles that can help you escape, if you can find and solve them.
- There has been a zombie apocalypse, and you have made it into the laboratory of some missing scientists who were working on a cure. You have to finish the scientists' work and find the cure before the zombies break into the lab and eat all of your brains.
- You are time travelers who have arrived in ancient Greece, where you discover that the ancient Greek gods have set up a trial for mortals that you have stumbled into. Solve their puzzles and escape or face their wrath.

Another great resource for coming up with escape room narratives is Hollywood. As long as you are using your escape room for personal, noncommercial purposes, you could lift entire plots from movies. Just make sure the solutions to your puzzles aren't given away in the movie itself!

Writing Tips

When working on a narrative, keep emotion in mind. It's more fun for players to be put in a situation that generates emotion.

Adding Emotion to a Plot

- Give your players noble goals.
- Create more serious consequences if players fail.
- Give players urgent time constraints.
- Reveal plot twists during the game with clues players find.
- Make the decorations more elaborate.

Creating characters that are compelling also helps an escape room plot. *Characters* here doesn't refer to your players; most people actually don't like to be assigned a character role or a backstory in an escape room. Part of the thrill is pretending like they themselves are doing something adventurous. *Characters* here refers to fictional identities created as part of the plot. You as the host might even have a character role. These pretend identities can be called *non-player characters*, or NPCs.

You want to create characters your players care about, whether the characters are antagonists (enemies to your players)

TIP:
Some of the details about the characters can be leaked out little by little as the players find and read things in the room. This can help prevent a host from having to read a long introduction before the game starts. Instead, the players can discover some of this information on their own, perhaps through a letter to someone, a message on a wall, a day count in tally marks, or pictures and photographs. These things can reveal characters' intentions, future plans, and backstory.

or protagonists (helping your players). For example, your narrative could involve your players escaping so they can hand something important to the police. Or your narrative could involve your players handing something to a character with a name and a bit of a backstory, like a hero trapped by a curse.

When creating escape room characters, keep their goals in mind. Do they ultimately want the players to escape or not? The answer to this question might also guide your puzzle types. A friendly character will leave puzzles that players are *meant* to solve, like messages written in code with an included decoder. On the other hand, the puzzles left by an unfriendly character *won't* be left to be solved, at least from that character's point of view. If you were writing an escape room with an antagonist like this, you might use a coded message without an included decoder (though you might need a simpler code that can be broken easily).

An escape room could have several characters with conflicting goals. How interesting would it be for your players to have to sort out on their own who is the antagonist and who is the protagonist, who is helping them and who has ulterior motives? Keeping goals in mind can help guide your plot and your puzzles and help you write strong characters.

Writing Compelling Characters

- Make your players care about the characters.
- Reveal small details about the characters' past lives, goals, or motivations.
- Create sympathy for an antagonist.
- Show what the characters are feeling. (For example, a letter left by a character could be written in shaky, ink-stained handwriting, as if they wrote it in a hurry or while they were scared.)
- Give your characters a reason for their actions and severe consequences if they fail.
- Keep characters' goals in mind.

The more details you add to your plot, the more information you'll have to convey to your players. So one very important thing to keep in mind is the amount of reading involved, whether it's something you're reading to your players or something you're leaving in the room for them to find and read themselves. Try to avoid multiple lengthy paragraphs. If you have lots of plot points or information to convey, try to do it in small, spaced-out intervals.

This can be hard! I often have to go through a lot of rewrites to trim my narratives down before they're ready. Even when I feel like I've trimmed down an escape room narrative to as lean as I can get it, when I test the room for the first time and actually read the introduction to my players, I cross out whole sentences as I realize what I'm reading is just too long.

Qualities of a Good Escape Room Narrative

- Doesn't involve too much reading
- Develops the story along with the puzzles and clues
- Sets up circumstances that generate emotion
- Has compelling characters in the narrative
- Incorporates the host and hints into the narrative
- Tries to minimize the requirement of suspension of disbelief
- Answers these questions:
  - Why are the players in the room?
  - How did they get there?
  - What do they need to do to escape?
  - Why do they need to hurry?
  - What happens if they don't escape in time? What's at stake?
  - Why are there puzzles and clues in the room?

These are just guidelines to give you some direction. A successful escape room doesn't have to hit all the points above. You can have a very successful escape room with a minimal narrative (you're trapped in a submarine and you have to escape!) or even no narrative at all. In the end the experience comes down to the puzzles and clues. You might even choose to sacrifice theme and plot for the sake of some really fun puzzles you want to include.

② Room and Decorations

In addition to giving some thought to your escape room's theme or story, you'll want to think about the actual room you'll use. There are some considerations you want to take into account when choosing a room.

Before we get into room choice, room prep, and decorations, I want to emphasize that there are levels of intensity when creating an event like this. You may want to host the escape room in your living room with a group of friends and not decorate much or even hide the clues. That's totally fine. Or you may want to host the escape room in your basement, remove all the pictures from your walls, cover everything in black tarp, and bring in black lights. That's totally fine, too. At the beginning, just give some thought into how much time and money *you* want to spend on your room and decorations. This is your room, customized to how you want it.

Now let's get into things to consider when choosing a room.

Size

You want your escape room to fit all of your players comfortably. This requires knowing how many players you'll have, or at least planning for the biggest group of people that might play. If you're aiming to create an authentic escape room feel, you also don't want your room to be too big. Ideally it should be the right size to fit with the theme and narrative. For example, a big open room might not work best for a prison-themed escape room. (This is why choosing a narrative that fits with your room is handy.) If you want to involve hidden clues, you also don't want a room that's too big for your players to search thoroughly.

If your room is larger than you want it to be and you don't have any other options, consider artificially making the room smaller with curtains, temporary walls, or tape on the floor. This creates clear boundaries for the game.

Number of Items in the Room

Part of the fun of an escape room is searching for clues. In a commercial escape room, players are often free to touch and search anything in the room. If we want to recreate that feeling in our DIY escape rooms, we need to have items in the room we are okay with our players searching through.

If you're serious about your escape room, you'll probably end up moving a lot of stuff out of the room—decor that doesn't match your theme, personal items you don't want your players to touch, even pieces of furniture. Then you might move other items in—decorations and props that do match your theme, the puzzles and clues you set up, etc. To create less work for you at the beginning, choose a room that's relatively empty.

For example, my favorite room in my house to host escape rooms in is our dining room. Even though the dining room has only three walls, I prefer it because there's not a lot of clutter to move out, there's plenty of space, and it has a big table that comes in handy as a work surface. I hang up a big curtain across the fourth wall.

Do you have a room chosen now? Great! Let's get it ready for your event.

Cleaning

To prep your room, start by moving items out. Move out anything you don't want your players going through or touching. When they play, it's more fun for them if they can search freely. If you have to keep saying, "Oh, don't touch that," or "Please don't search there," it inhibits their suspension of disbelief. So empty drawers, move out breakable knickknacks, and even take pictures off the walls.

After you have everything out of your room, I recommend doing a good cleaning. Once I hosted an escape room in a game room that hadn't been cleaned in a while. I felt very sorry for the players who searched the couches for clues and found only pieces of popcorn, missing socks, and dust bunnies instead. Oops. A good dusting and vacuuming would have prevented the embarrassing situation.

Think of all of this room prep as starting with a blank slate or canvas. Now you're ready to fill it with exactly what you choose—decorations and props to make your escape room feel more real.

Tape

Even if you move out everything you can, there still might be items in your room you don't want players to touch, like a heavy picture you just don't want to remove or a drawer that's too time consuming to empty. In this case, tape that's easy to remove can be your best friend (like masking tape or blue painter's tape).

Use this tape to mark anything you don't want your players to move or open. That way you don't have to give players a long list at the beginning of the game of everything not to touch; they can clearly see for themselves. (Depending on how serious you think your players are, you might even tape air vents and window latches!)

Use blue painter's tape to identify something players shouldn't touch or open.

Decorating

Once you've created your blank slate of a room, you're ready to think about the fun part—decorating. Remember, this can be as easy or as involved as you want it to be.

Decorating Tips

- One of the easiest ways to dramatically change a room is adjust the lighting. Try using lamps, strand lights, or colored light bulbs as opposed to normal overhead lighting.
- 3M Command hooks can be quite strong and attach temporarily to walls. They're great for hanging decorations on.
- Go small as well as big. Bring in small props that match your theme, like clocks, trash cans, knickknacks, books, etc.
- Invite your players to dress up or provide a few on-theme costume accessories for them to add as they begin the game (fake glasses, scarves, hats, rubber gloves, eye patches, etc.).
- Painted cardboard boxes can become crates, props, or artificial walls.
- Search the internet for inspiration.
- Shop at a thrift store, especially for historic themes. You'll be surprised at what you might find.
- Check out party stores and dollar stores for decorations.
- Use big pieces of fabric or sheets to create artificial ceilings.
- Another way to dramatically change the appearance of a room is to cover the walls, or even just parts of the walls. Hang props like pictures, calendars, or posters, and if you're serious you can use a variety of things to temporarily cover the walls. Creative options are fabric (including sheets and curtains), plastic (tablecloths and shower curtains), and paper (newspaper and wrapping paper). If you have a big budget and want to go all-out, peel-and-stick wallpaper is temporary and offers lots of pattern varieties.
- Don't forget the music. Music or background ambient sounds can add a ton to an escape room. Here are some ideas:
  - Search the internet for websites with ambient noise and tabletop game background music. Some sites let you create your own mixes.
  - Use soundtracks from movies that match your theme or music from suspenseful gameshows.
  - Create your own playlist on YouTube or Spotify. You might even find some playlists already created especially for escape rooms.

Some of your decorations might be props to add to the items players can search through in the room. Some decorations might be for looks only. It's okay to ask your players not to touch or search through these decorations. Use the blue painter's tape to keep boxes closed or to tape decorations or paintings to walls. I've also hosted escape rooms where I've decorated the walls quite elaborately and was able to just say, "Don't touch or search through the decorations on the walls." As long as these instructions to players can be given quickly and clearly, it shouldn't detract from the experience too much.

Finally, have fun with it! If decorating the room is something you're dreading, don't make it a big deal. If you think it's a lot of fun to decorate the room, go for it. An escape room is essentially a game. You want it to be fun—for you and for your players.

Hiding Places

When you're bringing decorations into your room, it might be helpful to think about hiding places. Some decorations can be a great source of hiding places. Some basic hiding place ideas are underneath and behind things like rugs, tables, and chairs; inside books; and hidden in or taped to drawers.

There are much more creative hiding places, and we'll talk about those more in part two, chapter fifteen. Some of the best hiding places can be ones that tie into the clues.

One tip I always give hosts is to make a list of where they hide *everything*. This is a lesson I've had to learn personally—multiple times! It might seem silly; you might think you'll remember where everything is. I promise, it's not always that easy, especially with lots of hidden clues. You don't want to be at the end of the game when the only thing

TIP:

When decorating, go for effect over authenticity. What matters most is the way your room feels as a whole. If some of the decorations are off by a couple of decades, as long as things are mostly on theme, the end result will be more impressive than a 100 percent authentic room that you could only find three or four decorations for.

TIP:

Make sure that wherever you hide your clues, they can be easily removed. I've hidden clues and realized after testing that they're really hard to get out (like a scroll hidden in a narrow-necked bottle—I eventually had to soak the paper to remove it). You don't want that to be something your players discover in the middle of a game. Preventing this simply involves testing your clues as you hide them.

stopping your players is a missing clue. All they need is a hint to find it—but you can't help them if you can't remember where you hid it! Be organized at the beginning and make a list on paper of where you hide everything. (There's a template for a hiding place list in the appendix on page 169.)

Part of the fun of hosting an escape room is seeing the "a-ha" moments your players have when they find or figure something out they've been puzzling over for a while, especially if they've passed over the clue once or twice before. Good hiding places can help create those "a-ha" moments.

Remember there's a fine line. A good hiding place can and should be difficult enough so that it's just a *little* maddening for players, but not so difficult that the players become frustrated and give up. Finding this balance will help create a fun, memorable experience. A good rule to follow is that the hiding places in your room should not be the most difficult aspect of the game. You want your room to be about solving puzzles more than actually finding the clues.

3

Creating the Puzzles

Now that we've talked about theme, plot, and setting, let's talk about actually creating a game. In fact, let's create a game! We'll learn about escape room structures in the process. Let's focus on structure alone for now and not worry about theme and plot.

Layers of Puzzles

When writing an escape room, it's often easiest to work backward. What is our players' final goal? To escape the room. So we need to lock them in. For this game, let's use a standard spin combination lock with three numbers.

01-03-29

All of our clues and puzzles must ultimately end in this combination.

How could we hide or code our combination? Let's start simple and write the whole combination in the margin of page 681 of a thick dictionary. (We'll write it small, in pencil, to keep our players from accidentally finding it.)

Now with the dictionary and combo, we've added another level of information to communicate to our players:

Merriam-Webster's Collegiate Dictionary, Eleventh Edition
Page 681

We could write all of this information on a card, lock that card in a box, and hide the key. To increase the difficulty, we could hide the dictionary in a bookcase with dozens of other books.

This itself creates a super simple, short escape room. We can make a diagram showing exactly what players will need to do:

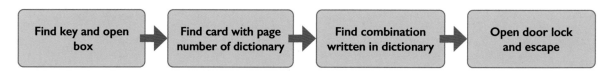

| Find key and open box | Find card with page number of dictionary | Find combination written in dictionary | Open door lock and escape |

The problem is, the puzzles all involve the same thing: searching and finding. There's not any puzzling or codebreaking involved. Searching and finding is a great aspect of escape rooms, but if it's the only aspect it's really just a scavenger hunt. It also makes the puzzles one-dimensional and less interesting.

How could we make the structure more complex? Instead of writing the book information as it is, we could scramble the letters.

MRIMRAE-ETBEWSRS
TCLOLEEAGI YOIADICNRT,
VETEHELN IIDONTE, APGE IXS
RDNUDEH DNA HEGTYI NOE

(Notice I spelled out the number so it could be scrambled along with the words.)

Now we've added another layer of difficulty to our escape room. Instead of simply finding and reading a piece of paper, our players have to do some mental work. Here's our new flow of puzzles:

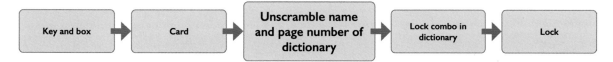

We could continue adding levels of puzzles to our escape room. Instead of leaving the card in a box locked with a key, we can leave it in a box locked with another combination, maybe a four-letter word combination, for example, BEAR. Then we can write down some clue words to help our players guess the combination.

We could hide the clue words in different locations in the room, if we wanted to incorporate even more searching and finding. To make sure it's not too difficult, it would be best if all of the papers and font looked the same, as shown in the picture.

Now we've created a strand of clues and puzzles that, simple as they are, could be the foundation for an escape room.

Linear Puzzles

This structure of puzzles is called a *linear* flow. Each clue or puzzle must be solved in order. After players find the hint words, they discover the combination BEAR. They unlock the box. That leads them to the scrambled words. After they unscramble those, they look for the book and page number. When they find it, they can open the door to the room. There's always one task to focus on at a time.

There are pros to linear escape rooms. They're very straightforward, so they eliminate confusion and are great for beginners. There are cons as well. For a large group, only one task at a time might leave some players without anything to do (only so many people can flip through the pages of *Merriam-Webster's Eleventh Edition* at a time). Experienced escape room enthusiasts might also find linear games a little boring.

So what to do? Instead of having puzzles that must be solved one at a time, we can create some complexity so different parts of the escape room can be worked on in any order, and so multiple parts of the escape room can be worked on at once.

Non-linear Puzzles

Let's go back to the beginning, or rather, the end: our combination of 01-03-29. What we really have is three bits of information, three different numbers. What if, instead of one string of puzzles that leads to the whole combination, we have three strings of puzzles that each lead to just one number of the combination?

We can reuse our first string of puzzles. This time, instead of writing the whole combination in the dictionary, let's just write the first number: 01. We will still keep our linear set of puzzles, only now it's part of the larger escape room. We still need to come up with a way to code the rest of the combination.

Take the next number: 03. How could we code it? We've done something with paper and locks. Let's change it up some. It would be great to add a physical element for a more tactile experience. For example, we could create a puzzle that involves counting some buttons and organizing them by some of their physical attributes.

| 15 buttons with four holes |
| 14 buttons with two holes |
| 7 buttons with words on them |
| 26 buttons without words on them |
| 9 red buttons |
| 4 black buttons |

These buttons can add a lot of variety to the puzzles in the room. If we mix the buttons up and players have to sort and count them, they're using their hands and handling small objects. The numbers involved are a natural opportunity to add math, like the equation below.

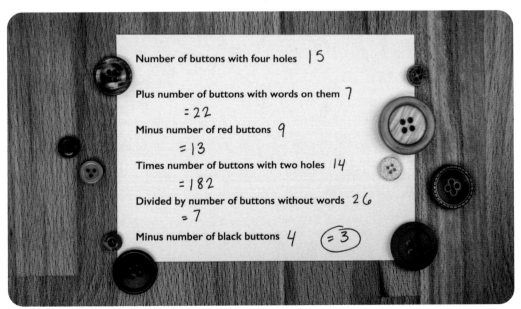

Number of buttons with four holes 15

Plus number of buttons with words on them 7
   = 22
Minus number of red buttons 9
   = 13
Times number of buttons with two holes 14
   = 182
Divided by number of buttons without words 26
   = 7
Minus number of black buttons 4   = 3

With a small jar of buttons and those instructions written out, we've added a layer of complexity to our puzzle, something players must solve to reach the second number of the combination (03).

Just like we did with the first puzzle chain, let's add another link. How else can we code the information we're giving the players?

What if, instead of just giving players the word problem, we cut up each line and don't tell players directly which order to put them in? Making players sort through this on their own would be near impossible, so it gives us a chance to incorporate another clue. We can use some sort of coded information, like braille dots, on the backs of the papers to tell players which order to put them in.

In the room somewhere we'll also want to include a paper that lists the braille numbers. It could be a fun little hint to draw a picture of a button on the paper. This gives players a clue that the braille numbers have to do with the button puzzle, though it does decrease the difficulty some.

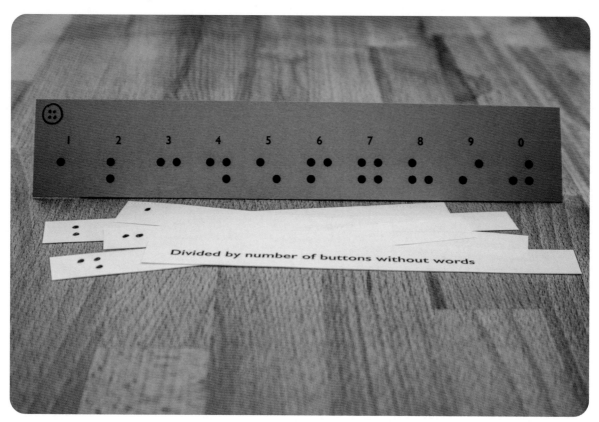

Now we have another chain of puzzles that lead to the second number of our combination, 03:

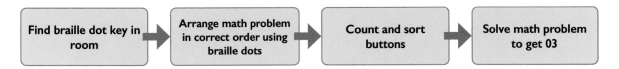

Just like the chain of puzzles that leads to the number 01, the chain of puzzles that leads to 03 is linear—each piece of the puzzle must be solved in order. But since we now have *two* chains of puzzles, our escape room as a whole is no longer linear. A couple of players could work on solving the first chain while a couple more work on the second chain.

Finally, we need a third chain of puzzles for the last number in the combination: 29.

Let's vary up the puzzles once more by incorporating something different, like a jigsaw puzzle. A puzzle like this provides an easy win for players because they know exactly what to do with it, though there is still work involved. A sixty-piece puzzle can take two adults about five minutes to complete and shouldn't be too difficult for an hour-long escape room.

We could write something on the back of the puzzle that leads to the number 29. We've already done a math problem. How about something with words? We can use a block of text, but every now and then we'll cApitalize a raNdom leTter, and when players put those letters in order it will spell "twenty-nine."

In cases like this, it can be fun to use text from something else like a poem, book, song, or movie, especially if it ties into the theme or plot. Here's a poem by Epes Sargent about the ocean (which is perfect because the puzzle I found is an image of the ocean). It also has enough letters to capitalize to spell out "twenty-nine." We'll just want to make sure we keep all the other letters, including the personal pronoun *I*, lowercase. In fact, the lowercase *I* is a good hint to players that capitalization comes into play.

a life on The ocean wave,
a home on the rolling deep;
where the scattered Waters rave,
and the winds their revels kEep!
like an eagle caged, i pine
on this dull, uNchanging shore:
o, give me the flashing brine,
the spray and the tempesT's roar!

once more on the deck i stand
of mY own swift-gliding craft:
set sail! farewell to the laNd;
the gale follows faIr abaft.
we shoot through the sparkling foam
like an ocean-bird set free,—
like the oceaN-bird, our home
we'll find far out on the sEa.

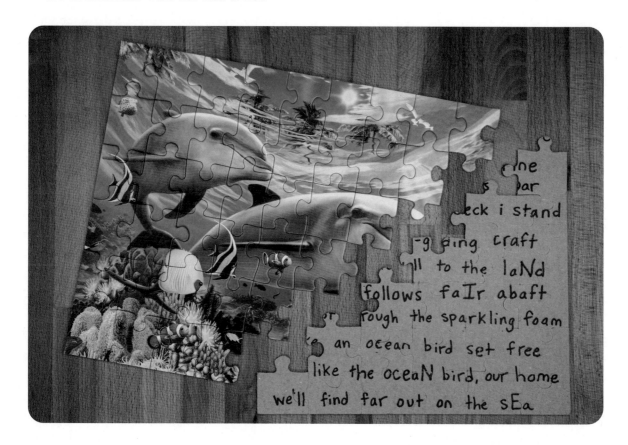

So far this puzzle chain to 29 is shorter:

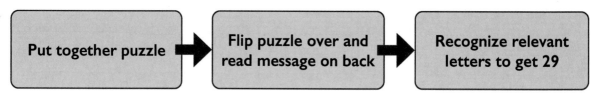

| Put together puzzle | → | Flip puzzle over and read message on back | → | Recognize relevant letters to get 29 |

However, since players have to put together a whole puzzle to get to this answer, it's okay to have a shorter puzzle chain.

TIP:

It's good to have a variety of puzzles in an escape room. For some tasks, it might be easy to tell what to do but take longer to do it, like assemble a jigsaw puzzle. For other tasks, it won't be apparent what to do right away, like seeing text that at first glance just looks like a poem. Once players have the "a-ha" moment and realize the secret clue, the answer comes quickly.

Let's take a look at our escape room as a whole now:

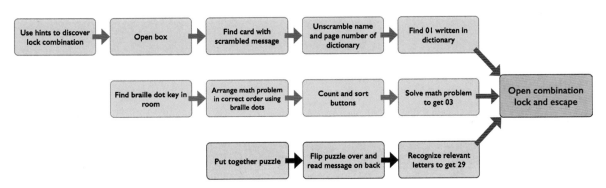

We've combined a mix of linear and non-linear puzzles. In doing so we've added quite a bit of clues and puzzles. Not bad! (Though this is still a simple escape room. Two adults could do it in as little as twenty minutes. Other escape rooms would have a more complex structure, with multiple mixes of linear and non-linear puzzles, and more difficult puzzles, as well.)

There is one more thing we could add. Once our players solve each of the puzzle chains and end up with a number, they're not going to know which order to put the numbers in on the final combination lock on the door. If we don't want to make them guess and check, we can include one last clue with some pictures that give players a hint as to the order of numbers in the combination.

If players pay attention to the clue and give it some thought, they should be able to deduce that the dictionary puzzle provides the first number in the combination, the button puzzle provides the second, and the jigsaw puzzle provides the third.

You may be wondering, "How do players know which puzzles in the room go together?" The answer is, well, they don't. Figuring out how to sort and make sense of the puzzles is part of the challenge. If we still want the structure of a non-linear escape room but want to guide our players a little more, we could color-code the parts of the escape room that go together. We could mark everything that ultimately leads to 01 with a green sticker, everything that leads to 03 with an orange sticker, and everything that leads to 29 with a blue sticker. This optional step still allows players to work on different parts of the escape room at different times but gives them a little more guidance to get started.

Non-linear vs. Linear

In choosing between a linear and a non-linear structure, the biggest consideration is probably the number of players. With a group larger than four players, consider a non-linear room. For a small group, especially for beginners, a linear room might be just what you're looking for.

Also take into account your desired amount of teamwork. Non-linear escape rooms can split up team members so not everyone is working together on one task. If your goal is to provide a really good team-building activity, you might not want players to split up. You might want them to all work together all the time. A linear room is great for this.

For larger groups or experienced players, a non-linear room might work best. Even a large group of players split up in a non-linear room are required to use teamwork.

If you have a large group of beginners, consider creating a non-linear escape room, but with added guidance like the sticker system mentioned on previous page. You could also group all the parts to one puzzle chain together in the room.

Side Goals

A spin combination lock with a combination like 01-03-29 lends itself well to a non-linear escape room. A keyed padlock with only one key might not work so well this way. Another way to bring in multiple chains of puzzles and avoid a strictly linear game is to work with side goals.

Side goals are things your players are trying to do in addition to escaping. In escape rooms I've written, side goals have included things like disabling security alarms, encrypting computer files, discovering key information, and bringing certain items out of the room.

We can add a side goal to our escape room. Let's say somewhere hidden in the room is a safe filled with money. If our players find it, they can keep the money *and* escape.

We can put the money (which could take the form of play money or fake jewels or a fake check) in a small, inexpensive safe. Then we'll use a black light and invisible ink to write the combination on a piece of paper. As an extra clue, we could draw a dollar sign in normal ink in one corner of the paper. This clues players in to the fact that this paper is important and not just trash.

We'll hide the black light, paper, and safe in different locations in the room, and then our side goal is set up. We could re-draw our escape room structure to include it:

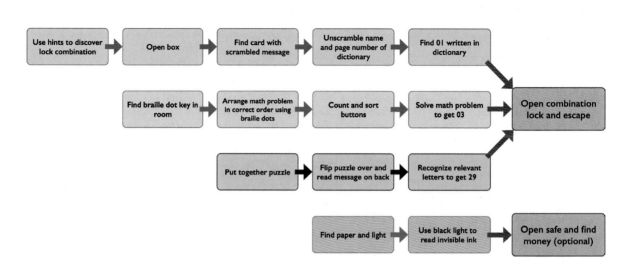

Notice that with this structure, the side goal is completely separate and optional.

An optional side goal works well for a single group doing the game once, especially if you're not limited on time. In those cases, the side goal is just for fun, and players will hopefully go for the extra goal because they want to keep having fun.

If you are running the game with multiple groups or if there is any sort of competition involved, an optional side goal makes declaring a winner hard. Once I ran a game that way with some highly competitive individuals. The players' main goal was to escape the room before the security guards came back. Their side goal was to find a first aid kit, realize its importance, and bring it with them. One team made it out first and didn't grab the first aid kit, while another team made it out a few minutes later and did. Disagreements followed. Tears may or may not have flowed. It wasn't pretty.

So, in the end, it's best if a side goal is required, especially for a competitive room.

Since you're the host and you make the rules, you can do this simply by saying so—say that players are not allowed to leave the room until they have the money. However, if you really want to make your side goal required, it would be better to build it into the structure of your escape room narrative. The fewer arbitrary rules we have to give out, the better.

If we want to do this in our current escape room scenario, we could put the jar of assorted buttons from the second puzzle chain in the safe along with the money. This keeps the side goal not strictly linear with the rest of the game, but it does ensure that players complete the side goal before they escape:

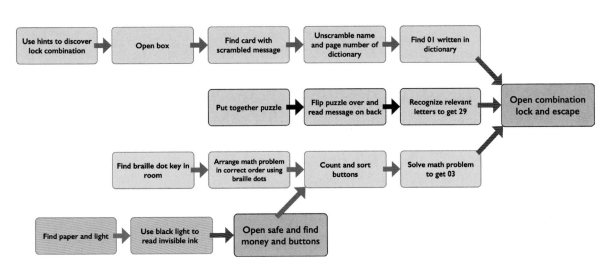

To do this with a side goal in your room, choose an object or piece of information players need to escape and don't make it accessible to them until they've completed the side goal.

Suspension of Disbelief

If you say the side goal is required when, according to the structure of the puzzles, it's optional, your players have the option to cheat. Part of the fun of a commercial escape room, however, is that you *can't* cheat, not even if you wanted to (unless you're an expert safe cracker or lock picker). That's why boxed escape games don't feel the same as a live escape room; there's nothing stopping you from opening the next envelope except your own free will.

The world isn't full of people who are out to outsmart and thwart escape rooms; on the contrary, people who do escape rooms are not going to want to cheat because they want to have fun. It just feels more realistic (and more fun) for them if they can't just open the next clue or walk out of the room. A sense of authenticity only adds to the excitement.

It comes down to suspension of disbelief. In a commercial escape room, players want to really feel like they're locked in a room. Many commercial escape rooms are great at creating this feeling. The amount of disbelief players feel as they go through the game is minimized.

In a DIY escape room, it's harder to create that authentic locked-in-a-room feeling, especially if we're going for elaborate settings, like an art museum or spaceship. Our sets aren't as elaborate and our puzzles aren't as high-tech. Players in DIY escape rooms have to use their imaginations more. As hosts of DIY escape rooms, we know this, but we want to help our players out as much as possible. That means there are fewer arbitrary rules and fewer opportunities to cheat (even if our players wouldn't).

Putting It All Together

Keeping track of all of your puzzles and clues can be a big task, especially if you're working with a non-linear structure. It's best to get organized and have a place to take notes, draw out puzzle chains, and scribble out and start over (because you will most likely go through a few drafts).

When writing an escape room, it's often helpful to start at the end and work backward, adding puzzles in layers to make the game longer and more difficult.

TIP:
Escape room structures can get quite long and involved, with lots of different parts and intersecting clue chains. My favorite way to organize escape rooms when I'm writing them is with a spreadsheet, which is especially useful if you're manipulating numbers.

Finally, the ultimate goal of an escape room should be to have fun! One thing that can quickly kill the fun is frustration. Non-linear games can be frustrating if players feel overwhelmed or confused. Linear games can be frustrating if players feel bored or if there's not enough to keep all players occupied. The best way to make sure your room isn't too frustrating is testing, which we'll talk about in the next chapter.

4

Difficulty

For escape room creators, managing the difficulty of the puzzles in a game is, well, difficult. There's a fine balance with difficulty. You want your room to be challenging, because the more your players have to work at a puzzle, the more rewarded they'll feel when they solve it. At the same time, you don't want it to be too hard or players will feel defeated if they don't escape in time or need too many hints. Coming up with the right difficulty level can be a real challenge.

This is an area where DIY escape room designers might have some advantages that commercial escape room designers don't. A commercial escape room is forced to stick to a schedule with a strictly enforced time limit. There also often isn't a way for commercial escape rooms to adapt the difficulty based on the group. In your DIY escape room, you may be free to take longer than an hour, and if you personally know the players, you have a greater chance of designing a room to fit their level of desired challenge.

If you're worried that you don't have enough control over whether players succeed or fail, realize that it's okay for players not to escape. It wouldn't be a challenge if that weren't a possibility. Players will still have fun as long as they feel the challenge was fair.

Here are some strategies to make sure your room isn't too difficult (or too easy).

Play Test

Play testing a game just means practicing—practicing the game with groups of people other than your intended audience (because players can only play through an escape room once).

After you've designed your room or as you're designing it, be sure to test it as often as possible. My first tester is usually myself, especially if I'm using physical props players will need to manipulate, like a jigsaw puzzle. Even on my own I can get a good idea of how long the puzzle would take players to put together. My second round of testing usually consists of my husband sitting alone at a table with all the puzzles spread out in front of him. It's not quite like the actual escape room where I would hide and separate the clues, but the test gives me enough of an idea to start making adjustments.

Play testing once is critical. Play testing more than once is even better. I understand it can be hard to gather multiple groups of people together to play test a game. Use whoever you can (spouse, friends, children, coworkers) and test as much as possible. Your escape room will only improve in quality.

Incorporate Hints into the Game

When you're designing your puzzles, try incorporating some hints into the structure of the game. If you've taped a clue to the ceiling, include a hint somewhere in the room that tells players to look up.

Here's another example. The numbers in the clue below correspond to elements on the periodic table.

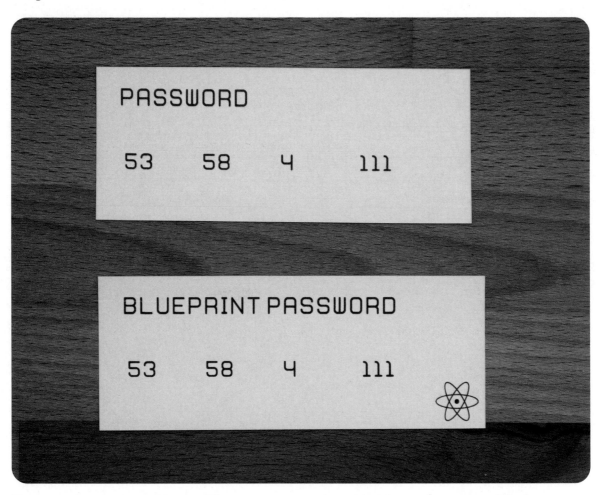

The same clue constructed in two different ways, one easier to decipher and one more difficult.

In the harder version of the hint (top slip of paper), the numbers are on a paper by themselves. In the easier version (bottom slip of paper), the paper has a small image of an atom.

The atom picture is a clue to players that those numbers have something to do with atoms . . . and hey, wasn't there a periodic table somewhere in the room? A-ha! Your players still get the "a-ha" moment of discovering something; they just have a little more guidance to get there.

Putting pictures on puzzles is a great way to incorporate hints into the game. So is color-coding puzzles that go together or grouping like items.

Characters in the game can also provide hints, perhaps with a clue in the character's name or backstory. For example, if you use a book to communicate a code, maybe a letter in the room can reveal that it's the character's favorite book.

Offer Hints as a Host

Every escape room I've ever seen or played comes with hints from a game master who is either in the room or watching from another room with a video feed. (For DIY escape rooms, since most of us don't have live video feeds in our house, hints are most easily given by sitting in the room with the players.) It's just so hard to predict what a certain group of players will struggle with, even if you have done a lot of play testing. There are several ways to incorporate hints into your game.

- Tell players they are allowed to ask for up to a set number of hints. This makes the hints valuable, and players will have to make careful decisions about when they should use them.
- "Charge" players for extra hints by adding to or subtracting from their game time. For example, you could charge three minutes for each hint. You would subtract time from players in a one-hour game (they would only be allowed fifty-seven minutes to escape instead of a full hour). You would add time if your players had an unlimited time to escape but they were comparing their

final escape time to other teams in a competition. In this scenario, if a team broke out at forty-six minutes but had to ask for an extra hint to do it, it would make their official breakout time forty-nine minutes.

- Make players earn hints by finding hidden hint cards or tokens in the room. Players must present you with one before they can get a hint. This could be worked into the plot; for example, each hint card could represent the phone number of a different fictional character that players can contact only once.

- Don't limit hints at all; give your players hints as often as they ask for them. (I recommend this strategy for children but not necessarily adults. Part of the fun of the challenge is trying to decide if it's time to use a valuable hint or not.)

As for methodology about giving the hints, this can be tricky. You don't want to give away too much or too little. The best thing to do is make sure you are watching the game diligently. As your players are going through the game, make mental notes of where they are and what would help them progress. Then if you're asked for a hint, you don't feel put on the spot.

Try not to give direct answers in your hint. One strategy is to format your hints as questions instead of statements. If there is something you know your players will just never figure out or have time to do, you could of course give your players the solution. When possible, try to avoid giving away actual answers. Your players will feel more rewarded if they do it on their own, even if they had guidance to do it. For

TIP:
Require that all players in the room be in agreement before they receive a hint. In the YouTube series "Escape!" by Geek & Sundry (which is a great series to watch for ideas, by the way), players are required to all call out in unison, "Helping hand!" before they're given a hint. You just want to make sure that one player doesn't ruin things for the group by getting a hint no one else wanted to take.

example, instead of saying, "Look in the filing cabinet," say, "Have you checked the filing cabinet?"

When offering hints, take into consideration how frustrated your players are versus how much fun they're having. If your players are clearly frustrated, that's no good. Consider offering a hint, even if they didn't ask for one. (However, *do* ask them if they would like a hint before giving one; unsolicited offers for hints are fine, but not unsolicited hints themselves.)

Choose the Right Types of Puzzles

There are two things that can make an escape room difficult: the quantity of the puzzles and the difficulty of the puzzles. There might be lots of little clues and puzzles in the room. This creates more activities for players to do and keeps them working quickly. There might also be fewer but harder puzzles and clues, ones that take more time to mull over. In each escape room it should really be a balance, but keep in mind which side you're trending toward and if that's the way you want to make your escape room challenging.

Choose the Right Structure

As discussed in chapter three, there's no doubt that the structure of the game (linear or non-linear) can dramatically affect the difficulty of an escape room, but it doesn't necessarily mean that a linear game is always easier. If there are some very difficult puzzles in the room, a strictly linear room might feel frustrating because players will reach a difficult puzzle and feel stuck on it, unable to make any progress elsewhere. Then they'll feel like they have to use up a hint or waste more time trying to solve the puzzle, perhaps getting more frustrated the longer they do. However, in a non-linear room, there will most likely be something else for players to work on at the same time so they can take a break from the difficult puzzle, perhaps taking turns with it and going back in a few minutes with a fresh perspective.

So both a linear and a non-linear game can feel difficult. It depends on your puzzles and your players. Speaking of . . .

Know Your Players

If you are planning a game for children at a birthday party, maybe you would rather err on the side of too easy than too hard. You would love to give your nine-year-old a victory on his special day. (We'll cover rooms for children more in depth in chapter six.)

On the other hand, if you're planning a game night for some brainy friends, you might want to err on the side of too difficult rather than too easy.

Also keep in mind how much time you want to fill. One reason commercial escape room facilities keep their rooms difficult is that they want players to feel like they've gotten their money's worth. Think, would you feel more rewarded if you got out of a room in twenty minutes, or if you got out just in the nick of time and enjoyed the entire hour your thirty dollars got you? It's probably better for commercial rooms to err on the side of too difficult.

As another example, perhaps you are in charge of entertaining a group of children for a full hour. If the room is too easy and they escape early, you're stuck for half an hour trying to keep groups of seven- to eleven-year-olds from chasing each other through the halls. (If that ever happens to you, I suggest playing the very fun game of "let's put everything back just the way you found it." Not that I'm speaking from personal experience or anything.)

Don't Let Players Get Stuck

A lot of puzzle-solving video games are engineered in such a way that players can't get stuck; that is, there's no way for them to work themselves into some sort of situation that they can't get out of without starting the level over. You can aim for this strategy in your escape room, too.

For example, in one of my rooms for children, I use clues hidden in balloons. The color of the balloon is important when looking at the clue inside it. However, if players rushed in and popped all the balloons without paying attention to which clue came from which balloon, they could easily get stuck. There's no way for them to go back and fix the mistake they've made. As the host, I would have to help them out of the situation. Instead, I indicate on the clue the color of the balloon it came from. Admittedly, this is less fun. It almost defeats the purpose of having colored balloons. Since the room is for children, I think it's an acceptable sacrifice to make.

Try to engineer your room in a way that players can't make irreversible mistakes. For example, don't write an important clue on a chalkboard and leave an eraser out with which players might erase your clue so they have some space to make notes. (True, this would not be very smart of your players, but you never know.) Perhaps you're using the arrangement of letter tiles on a Scrabble board to communicate a clue. Glue the tiles to the board so players don't mess them up.

This goes for any object with a location or placement that is meaningful or important. A common strategy for players in an escape room is to walk in, search for everything, and collect it in one place. Players doing this might easily forget which clue came from where.

If you want to make the placement of clues important, you should really stress this fact to your players so that they don't mess something up that can't be fixed without a hint. For example, if you're doing a detective-themed room and the placement of a book out on a coffee table is an important piece of evidence, you wouldn't want players to accidentally put the book back on the shelf and then forget where they found it. Let them know that location matters and that they should not move things all around in a desperate search. Then be ready to give a hint if they do get stuck.

Disguised Information

One thing that can make a puzzle in an escape room tricky is if a puzzle appears to be one thing when it's actually something else. For example, if you scramble the letters in some English words so they look like words in another language like Latin, your players might try to translate them when what they really need to do is unscramble them.

Nesalio
Sheppria
Shintepnum

ANSWER:
Sea lion
Sapphire
Punishment

Or you might use dots and dashes for something that isn't Morse code. If you have a block of text with certain words in red and you want your players to count the red words, your players might instead assume they need to come up with a phrase from the words in red; this could create some confusion for a while.

This disguised information trick might be a strategy you use to make your game more challenging, or it might be something to watch out for to make sure your room isn't too difficult.

Let Players Gauge Their Progress

A difficult puzzle is one with a lot of parts and no way to tell if each of those parts is done correctly or not until the whole thing is solved. In a puzzle like this, players might have 90 percent of the solution right and only 10 percent of it wrong, but in the end all they know is the answer didn't work and they can't do anything but go back to the beginning and start over.

The button puzzle given on page 23 is a great example of this. In that puzzle, players are given a set of buttons to sort and count. Once they know how many red buttons, black buttons, two-holed buttons, etc., there are, they are given a math problem to do with the numbers. The puzzle doesn't just involve a multi-step math problem—it *also* involves sorting and counting buttons. If players get to the end and realize the answer wasn't correct, they won't know whether to re-count the buttons or to check their math. They might assume they got one part of the problem wrong and double-check that first, only to work through the whole problem again and find that they're still wrong. You, as the host, may be biting your tongue in the corner, watching them re-count the red buttons when what they really need to do is check their math.

A puzzle like this, with a long string of things to do and no way to gauge success until the end, can increase the difficulty of the room. To make the button puzzle easier, we could make it less complicated (take out some of the buttons and some of the math steps) and compensate by adding smaller puzzles elsewhere in the room.

Math can be a tricky one with this. When working with numbers, try to be cognizant of how many opportunities there are for error along the way and whether players will know if they've messed up or not. There are ways to incorporate math and give players some way of gauging their success. For example, you might give your players a hint halfway through the puzzle and tell them they are looking for a three-digit number or tell them that the second digit is a two. If they get the math wrong, there's a greater chance of them knowing it before proceeding with the game and getting farther along in the process.

> **TIP:**
> If you do have a puzzle with many steps and you see your players have solved something incorrectly, consider stepping in with a hint early before they continue too far down the wrong path. That way they don't have to work the whole puzzle over again if they reach the end and the final answer doesn't work.

Offer Levels of Success

If you're worried about a game being too difficult, one way to address that is to give your players multiple ways to succeed. Side goals were discussed in chapter three, and levels of success work best in a non-competitive environment, but it is possible to give your players multiple goals that can be completed independently. The more goals players accomplish, the more successful they feel, even if they didn't finish every puzzle.

Avoid Red Herrings

Red herrings are clues that aren't clues at all— they are items or puzzles in the room that are there simply to mislead. There might be a pair of batteries that don't fit anywhere, numbers that show up under a black light that don't mean anything, a set of matching statues that seem suspicious but aren't, or just something that seems so random or out of place, it just *has* to mean something (but doesn't). Red herrings can quickly increase the difficulty of a room by taking up players' valuable time and brain power as

TIP:
You'll want to avoid any *accidental* red herrings, like a lot number stamped on the bottom of a chair from a factory. (Your players might see it and assume it's important information.) If an item does have something like a lot number, scribble over it or cover it up with tape.

they puzzle over something that in the end turns out to be useless. They can also increase frustration. Many players dislike red herrings that are only there to mislead. To keep the difficulty at a reasonable level, avoid red herrings.

Choose Numbers Wisely

Long strings of numbers can get overwhelming fast. If you're working with numerical passwords or math, anything over ten digits long will greatly increase the difficulty of the room. Providing a calculator (or letting players use their phones) makes math easier. Requesting that players do math in their heads or on paper, of course, increases the difficulty.

Don't Overdo Long Text

Just like lots of numbers, lots of text can get overwhelming. If you've hidden a clue among a whole newspaper you've created, your players will likely get a sinking feeling as they realize they need to comb through all of that text. Even if they don't need to read all the text, they still might feel like they have to. They might not know the difference between something that's relevant and something that's not. Rooms with lots of text just feel more difficult. Maybe you're going for that sinking feeling; just keep this in mind when designing your clues.

Check Your Technology

One way to control the difficulty of the game (and to make for good game design in general) is to avoid technological difficulties. Even if your technology is as simple as a combination lock, test your items to make sure they work well. A combination lock might get stuck. A laptop might go to sleep or run out of power mid-game. Running into a technological failure like this halfway through a game can not only feel difficult and frustrating for your players, it can also feel unfair.

Play Test Some More

I don't want to sound repetitive, but I do want to stress how valuable play testing a room can be. Especially if you are serious about your game or the stakes are high (like you're running it at work in front of your boss or for a whole summer camp), play testing is the best way to control difficulty. If you are limited in your testing opportunities—perhaps you are planning a game for children and you can only test it with adults—do the best you can. Even seeing adults play through the game will be helpful. If all you can do is test individual puzzles with friends over email, do that. Use who you have and test as much as you can.

I've tested rooms and found they were too difficult, and I've also tested rooms and found they were too easy. In testing you might realize that some of your hiding place ideas were too difficult. There might be too much reading. Something might be so obvious to you but be interpreted differently by your players. A puzzle might have too many pieces. Something might be frustrating because it takes too long. You may find that a small detail, like providing your players with tape to put a paper puzzle together, could go a long way.

Even if you can only test once, do it! It will be very valuable to you.

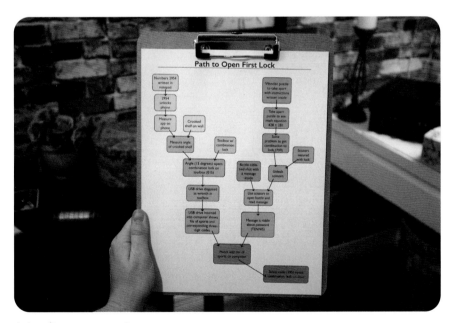

5

Hosting the Game

Once you have your theme picked out, your game planned, and your room decorated, you should be ready for your actual event. This event might be a birthday party, a team-building activity at work, a family reunion activity, a couples' game night, a youth group activity, or some other fun occasion. Whatever the event, being prepared will make everything run as smoothly as possible.

Before the Game

The most important thing you can do to ensure a successful escape room is test it, so hopefully you've been able to test your room as a whole or at least the puzzles in it as many times as possible.

Before the event, make yourself a handy document that sums up the escape room for you, like the diagram of puzzles from chapter three. Include answers to any problems and lock combinations.

A host's summary of a room.

Also have with you a list or map of where you hid everything. Keep these documents handy but in a place where none of the players will see them, like in a folder you hold.

As You Set up the Room

As you put your final puzzles in place, if possible, test them all one last time. This is especially important with anything involving technology. Check websites, the internet, passwords, power levels, etc. Also re-count any items that need to be counted, re-measure anything that needs to be measured, and just double-check everything to ensure your room runs smoothly.

As You Start

Decide at the beginning of your game if your players are allowed to use their smartphones or not. You might want to limit their access to the internet because you want them to rely on the information in the room, or they might need their phones to visit a certain website. Limiting access to the outside world can create a more immersive, authentic experience, so if you don't want them to use their phones, consider holding onto them for your players.

Give your players a chance to use the restroom or get a drink before they start so they won't feel like they have to stop mid-game. It's also important to wait to start the room until all players are present. It will be hard for someone to slip in after the room has been going on for a few minutes; other players will have to catch the latecomer up, and they won't want to waste their valuable time. Try not to start until everyone is there and ready.

Before the game starts, give your players any instructions, rules, and tips you have. Make sure all the rules are very clear (rules like no standing on the furniture, no peeling up blue tape, no lifting up the ceiling tiles, no punching holes in the walls—things like that). Also make sure your players know all the details about the hint system you're using.

If you are reading anything to your players at the start of the game, like a backstory that sets up the plot, try to memorize it instead of reading it. At least practice it a few times so you can read it with minimal glances at the paper

TIP:
Players like to see how much time they have left in the game. If you use a timer in your room, try to set it up somewhere your players can see it, too. One option is to display the timer on a TV screen or leave it on a phone in the corner. Otherwise, players will likely ask you multiple times how much time is left, which can distract them from the game.

and lots of eye contact with your players. Try to read with emotion; you're setting up what you hope will be a suspenseful game for your players. A long, dry introduction can have the opposite effect and bore your players instead of getting them excited to play.

As players enter the room, don't forget to start your background music or ambient sounds. It can really add to the tone of the room and completely change the mood. Also don't forget to start a timer. Even if your plot doesn't have a time-sensitive goal worked into it, players are going to want to know how long they took (especially if you're hosting the game more than once and there is any type of competition involved).

For Players: Escape Room Success Tips

- Work together and communicate as a team.
- Use your hints.
- Search thoroughly.
- If something seems confusing, move on; you might get more information on it later.
- Be organized as you collect, use, and complete puzzles.
- If you get stuck on a difficult puzzle, ask another player with a fresh perspective to try.

For Hosts: Acting Tips

- Don't speak more than you need to.
- Don't offer unsolicited hints.
- Memorize dialogue instead of reading it.
- Practice your lines with adequate vocal inflection and facial expressions (as opposed to a flat delivery).
- Project your voice so that you are loud enough for everyone to hear you clearly.

During the Game

I recommend sitting in the room with your players as they play. You won't make decisions for them, but they will appreciate having someone there for them if they get stuck. If you're in the room, you'll know exactly where your players are in the game and you'll be able to give better hints.

If your room has a plot, this is the reason it's handy to write yourself into it as a non-player character. Some examples of hint-giving NPC roles include a loyal butler, a helpful droid, or a team manager. Basically, you want to give your players an explanation as to why you're in the room and how you have hints for them. If you don't want to write yourself into an escape room plot or offer an explanation as to why you're in the room, that works fine, too. Your players will just pretend you're not there until they need a hint.

If you really don't want to be in the room, you need a way to monitor how your players are doing. If the room has a window, it may provide you with an opportunity to peek in periodically. A video feed would be a great way to monitor your players. In either of those situations, instead of entering the room to give a hint, one option is to stay out of the room and offer hints through a phone or walkie-talkie. Just be aware that your players won't want to spend a lot of time explaining their question to you; it's better if you already know where they are and what they need before they ask.

The hardest thing for me as a host during a game is keeping my mouth shut! You'll probably have a natural inclination to help your players, and it can be so tempting to jump in and provide a hint, especially if you've given yourself a role and permission to speak. Remember, some of the most rewarding moments of an escape room are the "a-ha" moments, and if you tell your players the answer or give them too much help at the wrong moment, you'll rob them of those.

One neat thing about DIY escape rooms as opposed to commercial escape rooms is that time doesn't have to matter as much. Commercial escape rooms have a time limit, usually one hour, which adds to the suspense. However, they're actually confined to these time limits; commercial escape room facilities need time to reset a room before the next group comes in.

It's possible that you as a DIYer don't have to worry about that constraint. In that case, you don't have to force your players to stop after one hour. As long as they are having fun and not frustrated, give them as much time as you have to finish the game. This is great because they can still feel like winners (and everyone loves to be a winner!).

Finishing the Game

Whether your players finish before an hour, you stop your players mid-game because the time's up, or you let them play until they escape, at some point the game will end.

There are some fun ways to wrap up a game, like by taking a photo. Many escape room companies do this. They have fun signs players can hold that say things like:

- WE ESCAPED!
- NAILED IT!
- WE DID IT!
- WE ROCK!
- WE SURVIVED [insert name of escape room]!

You might also provide a series of signs to hold if your players *don't* escape on time that have expressions like:

- So close!
- Almost!
- Whoops!
- Maybenexttime!
- FAIL

Even if you don't have multiple teams competing, prizes or awards provide a fun touch. Some awards could be for individual players, like "Most Clues Solved," "MVP," "Bossypants," or "Moral Support." Prizes could be for the whole team and could include things like candy or treats. Have fun tying your prizes into your plot or theme.

Finally, don't forget a debrief. Escape rooms can even feel incomplete if players don't get a chance to talk with each other (and with you) afterwards about their experience. The debrief doesn't have to be long; just take a few minutes to sum up the experience.

Possible Topics to Discuss in an Escape Room Debrief

- Tie up any plot points or solutions players missed.
- Let players fill each other in on puzzles and solutions they may not have seen.
- Talk about players' favorite parts.
- Talk about any frustrating parts.
- Go over things players would have done differently.
- Evaluate how well the group used teamwork.

Doing the debrief over themed refreshments is always a good idea. In one color-themed escape room for children, we had rainbow chocolate chip cookies afterwards. Cupcakes are always easy. An animal-themed room could be followed by cupcakes with animal figurine toppers. If you're hosting a sports-themed escape room, classic tailgate food like chips and dip would pair well. For an Old West room, serve sarsaparilla (meaning root beer with a homemade label) in glass bottles and old-time candy like licorice. A quick internet search will provide lots of ideas for desserts on various themes.

End-of-Game Checklist

- Congratulate your players.
- Remember to debrief.
- Take a fun photo.
- Serve refreshments (optional).

6
Escape Rooms for Children

Writing escape rooms for children is an intriguing challenge. It can be rewarding because many escape room companies don't have rooms specifically suited for children. They might even have a minimum age requirement such as twelve years. It's gratifying to be able to give the fun of an escape room to an audience who might otherwise not get to experience it.

Kids are different from adults in many ways, and escape rooms for a younger audience need to be adapted. Here are some tips to make your escape room for children a success.

Keep It Hands-On

Kids love hands-on activities. In one room I created specifically for children, I use Play-Doh, watercolor paints, and counting and sorting items. Try to incorporate activities other than ciphers on paper and combination locks. It can add a lot of variety and keep kids engaged, especially if there are different puzzle types that can appeal to a variety of interests.

Watch the Difficulty

As previously stated in chapter four, with children, it's probably better to err on the side of making your escape room too easy rather than too difficult. Adults can finish a challenge and fail and still have fun. Sure, kids can, too, but they'll have more fun if they actually escape.

When you're writing your escape room for children, keep your audience in mind. There's a big difference between nine-year-olds and thirteen-year-olds. If you have a large age range, try to include a variety of puzzles that suit different ages, like some decoding but also some searching and puzzle-assembling. There's also a difference between children who enjoy puzzles and riddles and children who . . . well, don't. Having a variety of puzzle types in a room can be helpful for this, too.

As discussed in chapter four, there are two things that can make an escape room difficult: the difficulty of the puzzles and the number of puzzles. In an escape room for children, it might be better to lean towards having more puzzles (and a greater variety of puzzles) rather than fewer, more difficult puzzles. That way, if players get stuck, they can get a hint and move on to something new and hopefully stay engaged.

Keep Groups Small

A group of twelve adults in an escape room together is quite a lot, and often too many. However, a group of twelve children in a room is *definitely* too many.

With children, smaller groups are better. You'd think that with more brains in the room they would be able to solve

TIP:

Be cautious when mixing age groups in escape rooms exclusively for children. For example, in an escape room with a few children who are thirteen and a few who are eight, the thirteen-year-olds will want to solve clues and work puzzles quickly and might not wait to explain things to the younger children, thus making the younger ones feel excluded or bored if they're not involved. Mixing age groups works best when there are also players mature enough to include those younger than them, like older teens to adults.

more puzzles, but I've found that larger groups tend to be less effective, especially with children. More children in a room can just lead to more confusion, noise, and chaos. People often work better together when there are only a few of them. With a smaller group, they will have more opportunities to cooperate and work together as a team. I recommend no more than six children in a room at one time.

Children escape best in smaller groups.

Don't Limit Hints

In games for adults, it can be fun to limit their hints, or to "charge" for hints by costing players for using them. I would not recommend this in a room for children. It would be good to have enough flexibility to be able to offer more hints to players if they need them. Above all, you want to avoid frustration and disinterest. Having flexibility with hints would be great for that.

When giving hints, still follow the guidelines to keep your mouth closed as much as possible, try not to jump in too quickly with hints, always ask players if they want a hint before giving one, and try to avoid giving answers outright. Children, just like adults, will feel most rewarded if they figure it out themselves.

Watch for Frustration or Boredom

The last thing you want in your escape room is frustration or boredom. An escape room should be a team-building activity and a chance to practice cooperation, sure, but at its core an escape room is a game. It should be fun, especially for children. Watch closely for signs of boredom in your players. If you notice their attention wandering or if they seem disinterested or are obviously frustrated, consider stepping in with a hint to keep them moving along.

TIP:

During the game, have a plan in case of frustration, like a few things in the back of your mind that you can step in with if things seem too hard. For example, create an easier version of one or two of the clues and keep them with you during the game. If children seem to struggle too much with the harder version, hand them the easier version.

Momentum is a good thing to keep in mind, especially with children, because they often lose interest quickly. If your players maintain momentum, they'll have fun. Getting stuck for a little bit can be good, because as they puzzle and think, they'll feel rewarded for figuring it out. You might also want to stretch and challenge them. However, if players get stuck on something long enough to feel like they've lost their momentum, that can be a bad thing.

Avoid Long Texts to Decode and Large Numbers

If you do use ciphers or coded messages in your game for children, I would keep them short. Kids could easily get bored or frustrated with a whole page of coded text. Instead, try to keep coded text to a few words or lines at most. Even a whole paragraph could be too long when working with kids. The same thing goes for large numbers; better to keep them short to avoid frustration.

Consider Players' Abilities to Restrain Themselves

I once ran a candy-themed escape room for children. It was so fun! The decorations were a blast to set up. I even provided a little candy bar and used some of the jars of candy as hiding places. In the game introduction, I hinted to players not to eat a lot of candy during the game and told them they would be rewarded with candy at the end.

I ran this room with several groups and learned some important lessons. For some children, like the older children (around age eleven), the candy was no problem. They enjoyed searching through it and might have sampled a few pieces, but it didn't distract them from completing the room. For other groups, like the younger children, the candy seemed to be a big mistake. There were children who wouldn't *stop* eating the candy. At least with some of my test players, the candy was just too big of a temptation.

In another escape room for children, I hid a clue inside a tub of Orbeez, or water beads (colorful marble-sized squishy, wet spheres). I thought it would be a fun, tactile experience for children to search through. It was! However, some children couldn't keep their hands (or *feet . . .* or *heads!*) out of the tub of water beads. The spheres started to disintegrate and it turned into a huge mess!

So keep your players in mind. A good general rule for escape rooms is to let your players complete the room on their own and not have to offer too much guidance or instruction. Constantly reminding players of rules can ruin the authenticity of the experience. If you are including an element in your escape room that could lead to a mess, make sure your players are responsible enough to respect the rules you set up.

It's also a good idea to limit the rules and make them as clear as possible. If there are rules in your room (such as "don't move the furniture," "don't climb on top of things," "don't remove the tape," "don't eat the candy," or "don't dunk your head in the water beads"), make them clear from the beginning. Repeat them. If you can work the reason for the rule into your plot, that's even better.

Make It Fun

While keeping players' ability to restrain themselves in mind, if you can surround your escape room with an engaging story, fun decorations, hands-on puzzles, and perhaps a treat or reward, it can help your young players stay on-task because they're having more fun.

7

Managing Large Groups

Escape rooms can be such a fun activity and opportunity for team-building, but one of the downsides is there's a limit to the number of people who can participate. I've seen twelve at most in a room, which is often too many; an ideal number might be closer to six. However, escape room events can still work for large groups. There are several ways to go about it.

Multiple Rotations

One way to handle an escape room with a large group is to cycle teams through the room one at a time. This method works well if you have a lot of time, because each team could take about an hour to play, and you will need time to set the room back up between teams. If you're hosting a company event split over several days, this could be the perfect option for you.

When running escape rooms with more than one group, competition always adds to the fun. Time each group and, at the end of the event, declare a winner: the team with the fastest escape time. Try creating a leaderboard so everyone can see who's in the lead.

Remember that when you reset the room between teams, you'll need to supply new copies of any puzzles or props that were written on or destroyed. For this reason, it might be best to use props that *aren't* easily destroyed. For example, if you freeze a key in an ice cube, you'll need a new key in a new ice cube ready to go for each room. It might be

Laminate puzzles you want to use more than once.

easier to hide your key in a different way. Create paper puzzles not to be written on so you don't have to print multiple copies. Laminating clues is an obvious way to do this, or design puzzles that can be solved on a separate paper and stress to your players not to write on them. Remember to provide plenty of scratch paper.

Multiple Rooms

If you don't have time to run all of your players through one escape room one group at a time, another option is to set up multiple copies of the same escape room. This comes with its own set of tips and challenges.

To do this, you will ideally have several rooms that are pretty similar in size, with a similar number of items in the room. Rooms in a school, an office building, a recreational building, a house of worship, or even your home could all work. Set up each room identically and let all teams play at once. You'll still want to time the teams, even though if you start all groups at the same time, you'll know immediately which team wins because they'll break out first. I've done an event like this where all teams were instructed to run to a central location as soon as they escaped. The first group to the location won.

If you're creating your escape room this way, you'll want to make each of the rooms as identical as possible. You'll need a copy of every prop and puzzle for each room you're setting up. Remember when we talked about hiding clues and making a list of where you hide everything? That's super handy when you're setting up multiple rooms. Create your list as you set up the first room, and then use the list to hide all the clues in all the other rooms in identical places.

> **TIP:**
> To create identical hiding places in each room, bring in outside props that create hiding places, like luggage, wastepaper baskets, or books.

You'll want to find identical hiding places, so if, for example, only one of the rooms has a window, don't use the blinds as a hiding place.

In addition to having multiple copies of puzzles and props, one for each room, you'll also need multiple hosts, one for each room. Depending on your room, your host might have quite a bit to do with the success of your team. If the host is written into the plot as a non-player character and has several lines to recite and hints to offer, the success of the teams will vary based on the host. For this reason, if your activity includes multiple hosts, train them before beginning to get them all on the same page as far as giving hints goes. Offer some rules about hint-giving and how much is too much.

The best way to structure a multi-room game like this may be with a host with a minimal role and some pre-made hints they can give out (like easier versions of the puzzles). It could go a long way in balancing out the fairness of the competition.

Another tip for multiple hosts is to make sure they're all familiar with the game, and the best way to do that is to have them play through the game themselves. If possible, run the game once with all your hosts beforehand. Then they'll all understand how the game works and be better able to give helpful hints. This will also give you another opportunity to test your room and make last-minute modifications accordingly, if necessary.

Multiple Groups in One Room

It is also possible to structure your game in a way to take up minimal space so multiple groups can play in one large room, like a conference room or gym. It is very doable to contain a whole escape room to a single table. Instead of hiding clues around a room, you'll just place them on the table or even use the table as a hiding place (tape things underneath the table or underneath chairs).

This way you can run several groups at a time in one room. Timing them is even easier this way, and you might not need an individual host for each table; one host might be able to manage two or three tables.

If you're having a team work at one table, smaller groups are best. Don't try to crowd too many players around a table. The more players there are in a group, the louder they might feel they have to speak to be heard, and the greater chance there is of other teams overhearing answers to puzzles. You don't want teams to be able to cheat off of one another. While it's likely that teams won't want this to happen and will hopefully keep their voices down, make sure you have enough space in your large room to provide plenty of distance between tables.

TIP:

When running an escape room with multiple teams in a large room, play some background music to provide a little more noise and make it harder for tables to pick up what their neighbors are saying.

You can even use a combination of the above methods, like multiple rounds in multiple rooms to get through everyone faster.

Keeping Score

You don't have to keep score by timing every team. Judge your audience; children might have enough fun playing through the room without being timed, especially if you're using different hosts who may or may not be a little subjective. It may be enough for them to simply escape.

With competitive adults, keeping score can add a lot of fun. When you're playing with multiple groups (whether they're playing at the same time or not) and keeping score, there are some important things to keep in mind:

- Have a clear method of giving hints. For example, use physical hint cards in the room so your host will easily be able to keep track of how many hints your players have used.
- If you're keeping score by timing players, remember to be as precise and fair as possible.
- In the case no one escapes in time, be prepared to judge on your own which team accomplished the most tasks in the room so you can still declare a winner.

Hosting an escape room for a large group might present its own challenges, but it's very doable and a fun way to provide a memorable and fun team-building experience for your group.

Part 2
Puzzle Ideas

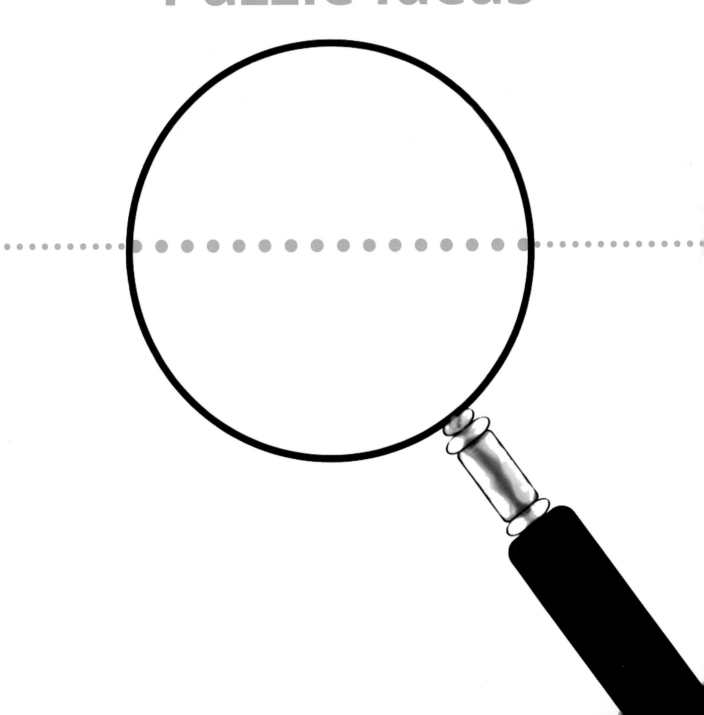

8

Overview

Themes, plots, and settings are all great fun to consider when it comes to writing an escape room, but the ultimate experience probably comes down to the actual puzzles and clues that make up the game. There is an endless supply of fun puzzle types and ideas. This part of the book will present plenty of them, but feel free to use your creativity and expand on any of these ideas.

Before we get into specific puzzle types in the next few chapters, let's go over some broad categories.

Escape Room Vocabulary

According to *Merriam-Webster's Collegiate Dictionary*:

- **Puzzle:** "a question, problem, or contrivance designed for testing ingenuity;" in this sense, any of the devices in an escape room could be called puzzles.
- **Clue:** "a piece of evidence that leads one toward the solution of a problem"
- **Challenge:** "a stimulating task or problem"
- **Hint:** "an indirect or general suggestion for how to do or solve something"
- **Code:** "a system of symbols (such as letters or numbers) used to represent assigned and often secret meanings"
- **Cipher:** "a method of transforming a text in order to conceal its meaning," or, "a message in code"
- **Cryptography:** "the enciphering and deciphering of messages in secret code or cipher"
- **Encode:** "to convert (a message) into code"
- **Decode:** "to convert (something, such as a coded message) into intelligible form; decipher"

Creating Puzzles

We've talked about testing whole rooms, but it's also important to test individual puzzles, whether they're jigsaw puzzles, crosswords, stacks of blocks, or unlocking a cryptex. It's very important to test these individual puzzles as you're planning them. Often this testing can be done only by you (or with another friend if you want a second opinion). When you're testing your puzzles, keep these things in mind:

NOTE:

In cryptography, the terms *code* and *cipher* have technical definitions and mean different things. However, according to *Encyclopædia Britannica*, the term *code* "has been frequently misapplied and used as a synonym for cipher . . . in fact, many historical ciphers would be more properly classified as codes according to present-day criteria." Since the distinction between *code* and *cipher* has been messy historically and we're not cryptographers anyway, it's not one I'm going to worry about.

- Is the puzzle doable? Will the solution be easy for your players to replicate?
- Can the puzzle be done in a reasonable amount of time? More than ten minutes on any single task is most likely too long.
- Is the challenge likely to cause frustration? If the answer is yes, consider modifying it.

Self-Verifying Puzzles

In most commercial escape rooms, things happen automatically, whether it's as simple as a combination lock opening or as elaborate as a door with magnets activated by putting weight on a scale. In either case, when players find some sort of solution, they know immediately on their own whether they did it correctly or not because something happens automatically; the puzzle itself verifies the correct answer.

As DIYers, we don't usually have fancy magnetic locks and computer chips at our disposal. But the types of puzzles where players know on their own whether they got the right answer or not are still the best way to create an authentic escape room feel.

Here are some items a DIY escape room can use to create self-verifying puzzles.

- Locks
- Jigsaw puzzles
- Password-protected computers and phones
- Password-protected documents, websites, or email accounts

There are other ways to create self-verifying puzzles, but it does take a lot of creativity, especially if you are limited by a theme (like a historic setting that wouldn't lend itself to computers or technology). For this reason, if you are extra concerned with having self-verifying puzzles, you might want to choose a modern-day theme for your escape room. Remember, the goal is that players know on their own when they've solved something correctly.

Host Feedback Puzzles

It is possible that, in your escape room, you might not be able to have only self-verifying puzzles, perhaps for variety's sake (you don't want to overdo combination locks) or for your theme or plot (it could be ancient China when computers didn't exist). In that case, your only other option is to tell players yourself when they've done something correctly.

This is less like a commercial escape room and does take a bit more imagination. If you are able to work host feedback puzzles into your escape room, try to do it creatively. The best way to do this is to incorporate the host (and the reason he or she is providing answers) into the plot.

In one of my escape rooms, I disguised the feedback-giving host as a character in the narrative. Instead of the host being just a host, I had the host play the role of a helpful droid. When players found the solution to a puzzle, they gave the answer to the droid who "fed the information into the ship's computer" and got feedback to pass on to the players if the answer was correct or not.

When players complete a host feedback puzzle, the host either gives them a piece of new information they need (like a lock combination), or permission to go ahead with a task (like open a box or access something new). The host might even give players something physical, like a key to a lock.

Though host feedback puzzles do take more imagination on the players' part, these puzzles can be just as fun. They also open up a huge range of possibilities, offering players the chance to do all sorts of things to escape the room.

Tasks Players Could Do for Host Feedback

- Utter a spell
- Eat something specific
- Build a human pyramid
- Stand in several different parts of the room or touch different parts of the walls in a room at once
- Sing or play a song
- Make a human chain across the room to conduct electricity
- Concoct and drink a potion
- Complete a team-building task
- Turn on a light or lamp
- Build a structure
- Put on a certain outfit or article of clothing
- Measure their own height or weight
- Correctly complete a hand-eye coordination task
- Interact with the host (give the host a potion, help the host regain lost knowledge, etc.)

TIP:

The best way to work host feedback into your plot is to make the host someone helpful but not an authority; kind of a go-between that communicates with something or someone the players can't, something that needs the players' help or will help the players if they meet certain conditions. If the host, according to the plot, does have the answers, there needs to be a reason he or she isn't giving them (for example, for the players' own safety or to test their knowledge).

Ways to Work Host Feedback Puzzles into a Plot

These are all things the host could pretend to do.

- Talk to a computer
- Leave the room and talk to someone else
- Email someone and receive a response
- Consult a rulebook to make sure something's done correctly, like hot-wiring a door (Note: The fictional rulebook would have to be constructed in such a way as to not give the host the answer outright; perhaps it's too big and cumbersome to look through without the players giving the host the exact page number to check.)
- Communicate with a ranger station or base camp, maybe through a made-up code that only the host knows how to use
- Interact with a pretend panel on the wall (or with a tablet computer)
- Communicate telepathically with someone or something
- Use a language only the host knows how to use
- Talk to the guys in the truck down the street doing the stakeout (if the players are burglars or spies)
- Act as a priest to a Greek god or the spirit of a pharaoh trapped in something
- Have a spell cast on the host, making it so the host can't give away a right answer but can verify one
- Talk to a lookout to make sure the authorities aren't coming

You may also want to use host feedback puzzles in your escape room but not work them into your plot; perhaps you don't even have a plot. That's okay. When your players complete a puzzle or do something correctly, just give them the answer or permission to move ahead without an explanation.

Host Feedback Puzzles that Feel Self-Verifying

It is possible to use host feedback puzzles that *feel* like they reveal the answer automatically. If your players solve something and you can trigger a response discreetly, your players might not even realize that you have done so. Technology can be very helpful in situations like this. For example, during the game you could hold a concealed phone with you. When players do something correctly, like stand in four corners of the room at once, project or stream a new clue from your phone to your TV. From your players' point of view, they completed a task and received the answer automatically. Other options include playing something over Bluetooth speakers, sending an email to the players, turning on a light switch, or using a remote to turn on a TV.

Answers Don't Have to Matter

One neat thing about host feedback puzzles is that the answer doesn't necessarily have to matter. For example, in a room I've run, I wanted my players to build a long chain of plastic straws. To create a reason for this, I required an answer to a problem after they built the chain, but I really didn't care what the answer was; I just wanted them to figure out they needed to build the chain. The sneaky thing is that the players didn't have to know that I didn't care what the answer was. When the players in my room built the chain of straws and gave the answer to the host, the droid just said, "Yes, that worked! That's the password the computer needed. Now the computer is reprogrammed and we can open the blast doors!"

As another example, have you ever seen bath bombs for kids with a surprise toy hidden inside? How fun would it be for your players to have to dissolve a bath bomb to discover to a clue? The problem is, if you're trying to create a self-verifying puzzle, you would want to use whatever's inside the bath bomb as an answer, and you might not have any way of knowing if it's a duck or a starfish inside the bath bomb if you purchase it from a store. However, with a host feedback puzzle, it's okay; during the game when your players dissolve the bath bomb and find the figurine and tell you, "Duck! It's a duck!" you can use whatever host feedback device you've worked into your plot and say, "Yes! That was the password! It worked! Now I can give you this information . . ."

Optional Puzzles

Another possibility host feedback puzzles allow is the opportunity to create optional puzzles. In the YouTube show *Escape!* by Geek & Sundry, there are optional standalone puzzles marked by an hourglass icon. If players complete them, they are given five extra minutes to escape. The only way to add these extra minutes to the players' escape time would be for the host to do it manually, so this is where host feedback comes in.

It could be fun to offer this additional challenge to your players, and to provide them with a choice: should they spend time on the quick optional puzzle and gain extra time, or should they focus on the required tasks at hand? If the extra-time puzzles are quick, it could give the players an easy win, a surge of confidence, and excitement to keep going. If those puzzles are too long and confusing, however, that could lead to frustration and indecision.

Tips for the Host

Even with host feedback puzzles, you want the escape room to be a challenge your players complete on their own and find the answers to on their own. Still look at yourself as a host or game master and not as one of the players, even if you have given yourself permission to talk with and interact with the players. Remember not to solve anything for them.

TIP:

Host feedback puzzles work well when the host can do a little role-playing. You don't have to be an experienced actor, but give your role in the game a little practice or thought and try to make a convincing performance for your players.

Now that we've covered broad puzzle types, we can talk about specifics. Each of the next chapters covers a different type of puzzle. Host feedback puzzles will be marked with an icon to make them easy to identify (or skip, if you are not interested in doing host feedback puzzles).

9
Math and Numbers

Since numbers are so often used in things like lock combinations, finding ways to manipulate numbers is an easy way to add layers of puzzles to an escape room.

Counting

The simplest way to incorporate math is counting—have your players count how many there are of an object and make that number relevant. Players could count a variety of things: everything in the room that's blue, all the pieces of fruit, the spots on a ladybug, or all the bold words in a block of text. Players could also search for the objects before they count them if you hide the objects or even just spread them around the room in inconspicuous places.

If you want to increase the difficulty, make one of the objects slightly different. For example, if you want players to count all the apples in the room, spread a few apples around the room or include a bowl of fruit, *and* have a painting on the wall of a still life with an apple in it. Players would have to notice the apple in the painting and realize they should count it, too. (This can be fun, or it can be frustrating; try to gauge your audience and your desired difficulty level.)

Another thing players can do before they count is sort. In a toy-themed escape room, players could sort LEGO bricks by color, count them, and solve equations with the numbers they obtain.

Having players count letters or words you call attention to is a good way to increase the difficulty of a room. Players will most likely expect to unscramble or create a message from the letters or words you specify. It might take some thought before they realize they should count them. This is a good puzzle if you want to create a difficult challenge, as discussed in chapter four.

TIP:
Remember, when you're incorporating counting, watch the number of items. Larger numbers can increase the difficulty (and the opportunity for error).

Math

Once your players obtain some numbers—whether by counting or some other means—they can do some basic math problems with them. Since escape rooms are meant to be tests of teamwork and problem solving, I would stick to easy math like addition, subtraction, multiplication, and division, so that your room is more universal and accessible to most people.

As discussed, a reminder on length: the bigger your numbers get and the more steps your math has, the more opportunities there are for error and the more difficult the puzzle gets. With longer math problems, try to include ways for players to check their progress halfway through, like a hint that they're looking for a multiple of five.

Ways to Add Numbers to Puzzles

Aside from simply counting things, there are other ways to encode numbers into your escape room. Adding a number in any of these other ways is just another step, another puzzle for your players to solve. (Number types and codes on page 72 marked with an asterisk should include a key for players in the room. These can be found in the appendix.)

- Clocks—Remove the batteries from an analog clock and set the hands to a certain time you wish to communicate. The shape of clock hands can also be used to communicate the numbers one through twelve, which is fun because it might take some thought for players to recognize and might provide a good opportunity for a built-in hint.

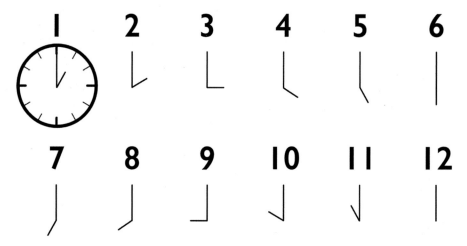

Use the shape of clock hands to creatively disguise a number.

A tiny clock charm is a fun hint that the lines drawn on the paper correspond to the hands on a clock.

ANSWER:
3, 10, 7, 5, 2

- Phones—Give players a message written in letters and have them use the numbered keys on an old phone to identify which numbers match the letters.

The letters on an old phone can be used to convert a message in letters to a password in numbers.

- Talley marks
- Letters—Spell numbers out in words. Those words can then be coded with any code or cipher in chapter ten.
- In text—Hide numbers in a block of text by replacing some letters with numbers: app1es, sup3r, ba5ement, w0nderful.
- Seven-segment display—The type of numbers that are used in digital clock and calculator displays provide lots of ways to creatively illustrate the shape of a number. Anything from toothpicks to popsicle sticks to two-by-fours (or anything else creative) can create the numerals.

Seven-segment display numbers (4, 3, 6, and 3) created with popsicle sticks might take some observation to notice.

- Roman numerals—These can be a tricky way to disguise letters as numbers and vice versa.* (See page 167 in the appendix for the key.)
- Binary—This is the way digital electronics code numbers in ones and zeros.* (See page 163.)
- ASCII Code—This code is used in electronic communication and would be great for a computer-hacking themed room.* (See page 163.)
- Morse code* (See page 165.)
- Braille dots—These patterns of raised bumps on a page were created so the blind can read.* (See page 164.) *A note on numbers in braille: The dot patterns for the numbers zero to nine are actually identical to the letters A to*

J. There is a special marker in braille to indicate when a number is being used. To reduce complexity, I recommend not using braille numbers and braille letters together in the same room.

Objects with Numbers

Physical objects can also be used to communicate numbers that are part of solving a puzzle. If you want players to add three numbers together, you could write the numbers on paper, or you could include three billiards balls in the room and give players instructions or a hint that they should add them. Objects like these are fun to include because they're physical, provide variety, and could tie into your theme. If you don't include the object itself, use a photo, image, or description of it. Here are some other ideas.

- Dice (mark one side)
- Playing cards
- Scrabble tiles
- Uno cards
- Measuring cups
- Money
- Percent cotton or polyester in a shirt
- Weight, length, height, and width of items
- Volume (in ounces, quarts, gallons, liters, milliliters, etc.)
- Dominoes
- BINGO balls or squares
- Raffle tickets
- Clothes or shoe sizes
- Matchbox or Hot Wheel cars or other toys with numbers on them
- Drill bits
- Encyclopedias
- Dart boards
- Thermometer or thermostat
- License plates

- Checks
- Flight numbers
- Graph coordinates
- Calendars
- Page numbers of books
- Makes and models of cars
- School grades (report cards, quizzes, or tests)
- Miles/kilometers between points on a map
- Serving sizes of food
- Prices of items
- TV channels
- Radio stations
- Acres of land
- Arrival/departure times
- Vertices, edges, and faces of 3D shapes
- Video game levels
- Game scores
- Addresses, road numbers, ZIP codes, or apartment numbers
- Phone numbers
- Speed limits
- Longitude and latitude
- Dates
- Anything you can give an ID number to (students, employees, etc.)
- Carats of diamonds or karats of gold

TIP:

If you use one of these items to communicate a number, make sure the number is fairly apparent and won't be skipped over or ignored by your players, or that you include a good hint to help players notice it.

10

Codes, Ciphers, Letters, and Words

Along with numbers, coding or representing letters and words is something almost every escape room could use. There are many ways to communicate letters and words, much more than just ciphers where you replace each letter with a different symbol, number, or letter.

Replacing Letters with Other Letters

Cipher Wheel

A cipher wheel consists of two attached disks that can be rotated freely. Letters on one disk line up with symbols (or more letters) on the other disk, representing which letter or symbol should be substituted for the actual letter to create the coded text. If your players have a cipher wheel, you need to communicate to them exactly how to position the disks, and then the wheel will give them an easy way to decode a message. Cipher wheels can be purchased or even homemade with paper.

A cipher wheel is used to encode and decode messages.

Caesar Cipher

In a Caesar cipher, letters of the alphabet are substituted with other letters by simply sliding the alphabet down a certain number of spaces. For example, if you shift the alphabet one space, A becomes B, B becomes C, C becomes D, and so on until Z becomes A. That way the word SNEAKERS would read TOFBLFST. The alphabet can be shifted as many as twenty-five spaces. A cipher wheel pairs great with this type of cipher.

Keyword Cipher

The keyword cipher is a lot like the Caesar cipher, but instead of communicating a number of spaces shifted, you communicate a keyword. For example, if the keyword is PSYCH, you would create the code as follows:

Letter in message	A	B	C	D	E	F	G	H	I	J	K	L	M	N	O	P	Q	R	S	T	U	V	W	X	Y	Z
Replaced with	P	S	Y	C	H	A	B	D	E	F	G	I	J	K	L	M	N	O	Q	R	T	U	V	W	X	Z

When creating the code, you list the keyword first, so A is represented by the first word in your keyword, B is represented by the second, and so on. After the keyword, just start the alphabet from A to Z, but skip any letter already represented in your keyword (so you'll notice that in the example above, G is represented by B, and H is represented by D instead of C, because C was used in the keyword).

Using the above cipher, the word PINEAPPLE would be encoded as MEKHPMMIH.

A keyword cipher works when the keyword contains letters at the very end of the alphabet. Otherwise half of the alphabet ends up being the same, as in this example with the keyword BAG:

Letter in message	A	B	C	D	E	F	G	H	I	J	K	L	M	N	O	P	Q	R	S	T	U	V	W	X	Y	Z
Replaced with	B	A	G	C	D	E	F	H	I	J	K	L	M	N	O	P	Q	R	S	T	U	V	W	X	Y	Z

Atbash Cipher

In the Atbash cipher, the letters of the alphabet are simply reversed. So A becomes Z, B becomes Y, C becomes X, and so on.

Columnar Transposition

In a simplified columnar transposition cipher, you write your text in a block and code the text by reading down in columns instead of across in rows. For example, let's start with the coded text of NOTS ANRU TAER ILAE. To decode it, we are instructed to write the coded words as four equal columns (with the words going down) and place them next to each other:

N	A	T	I
O	N	A	L
T	R	E	A
S	U	R	E

Then if we read the message left to right instead of top to bottom, it spells NATIONAL TREASURE.

If your message doesn't have an even number of letters, add an X (or several) to the end of the message so it fits into equal columns, like the way THE GREAT ESCAPE is coded here:

T	H	E	G
R	E	A	T
E	S	C	A
P	E	X	X

Transposition

You can always change up letters simply by scrambling them. When you take a phrase and scramble the letters to form new words, it's called an anagram. There are generators online where you can easily make your own. Can you unscramble this one?

LIMB OMISSION SPIES

ANSWER:
Mission Impossible

Scrambling the letters in words so that they look like other words can create a tricky puzzle. To make it easier, reverse the letters of a whole string of text:

YTITNEDI ENRUOB EHT

ANSWER:
The Bourne Identity

Or scramble individual words or spell individual words backward.

Replacing Letters with Numbers

A1Z26 Cipher

In this simple cipher, each letter becomes the number that marks its position in the alphabet. So A becomes 1, B becomes 2, C becomes 3, all the way to Z, which becomes 26. This type of cipher can often be decoded by players without any key or hint because it's fairly obvious. When you write the coded message, be sure to include a space between each number, because some letters are represented by one digit and some by two.

Polybius Square Cipher

This cipher was invented by the ancient Greeks. It's a way of representing each letter of the alphabet by a two-digit number.

	1	2	3	4	5
1	A	B	C	D	E
2	F	G	H	I,J	K
3	L	M	N	O	P
4	Q	R	S	T	U
5	V	W	X	Y	Z

To find out the number that represents a letter, just read the coordinates of the space in the grid, with the left coordinate first and the top coordinate second. So A becomes 11, B becomes 12, H becomes 23, and so on. (The letters I and J are usually combined, so both would be represented by 24.)

Since each letter is always represented by two digits, you can code a word as a big block of numbers, without breaking the word apart by letter (unlike the A1Z26 cipher). This increases the difficulty if your players aren't aware at the beginning that they're using a Polybius square cipher and are instead expecting something like the A1Z26 cipher (or some math). The blocks of solid numbers can seem confusing.

4344421133221542 442324332243

Common Letters to Numbers

To create an easy cipher for children, replace just the vowels (A, E, I, O, U) with numbers.

Letter in message	A	E	I	O	U
Replaced with	1	2	3	4	5

Then the message A CHRISTMAS STORY would read 1 CHR3STM1S ST4RY. As you can see, it's very easy to decode.

To make it more difficult, code some or all of the most common English letters (E, A, R, I, O, T, N, S, L) with numbers 1 through 9. Assign the numbers alphabetically to make it easier (1 CH7389M18 8967Y), or randomly to make it more difficult. Assigning the numbers randomly might make it *so* difficult it would be impossible or very time-consuming to decode without a key, so consider providing a whole or at least partial key.

ASCII Code

This code used in electronic communication can represent letters as numbers. For example, the letter A is represented by 65. See page 163 for the key. (Don't forget to include the key in your room, too!)

Replacing Letters with Symbols

Symbol Cipher

Choose any set of twenty-six symbols or pictures you want and assign a letter to each one. Code your message by replacing each letter with the corresponding symbol. Your players would then need a key or some sample translated text to decode the message.

A sample symbol cipher, a hieroglyphic-inspired alphabet.

This is a fun cipher to customize to your theme. You can choose pictures of anything you want, like music notes and symbols for a music-themed room.

Pigpen Cipher

In this cipher, the letters in the alphabet are arranged around shapes and dots that give each letter a unique symbol. Pigpen is fun because the key itself takes some deciphering if you aren't familiar with it. (Don't forget to include the key in the room!)

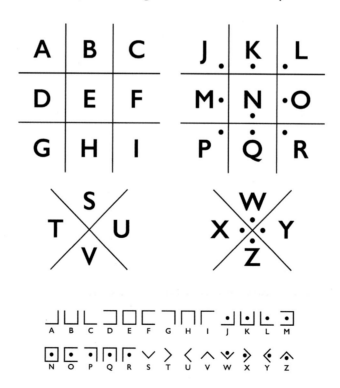

Can you tell what this coded pigpen message is saying?

ANSWER:
War Games

Braille

Use braille dots to communicate a message. For added fun, used dots punched with a pen to create a tactile feel (though I would still let your players rely on their sense of sight). Another idea is to make the braille dots extra-large. They might be harder to recognize that way and increase the difficulty. (See page 164 in the appendix for the key.)

Morse Code

Morse code is fun because it's versatile. Code something in Morse code with dots and dashes written on paper, with longer and shorter beeps, or even with a light bulb flickering on and off for longer and shorter segments. (See page 165 in the appendix for the key.)

There are more ciphers, some of them much more complex. A simple search of "types of ciphers" online should provide plenty of options for you.

In general, it's a good rule to have your players

TIP:
Decoding a secret message should only be one part of a larger escape room. Even if the decoding is relatively easy to do, you don't want it to be too time-consuming. If decoding something takes longer than ten minutes, consider simplifying the clue.

be able to figure out how to solve a clue, puzzle, or code on their own, without a lengthy tutorial on how to do it. If you want to use a keyword cipher but would need to give your players a lesson on how to solve it first, consider another type of cipher instead, one they can more or less figure out on their own, or give them the lesson before they enter the room.

If you do want to teach players how to solve a cipher they might not be familiar with, instead of including a tutorial, try including a sample of coded and decoded text in the same cipher somewhere else in the room. Just an example of some decoded text could be enough for players to decode most ciphers. This could work well with a columnar transposition cipher or a Polybius square cipher, for instance. An example of coded and decoded text is a good way to avoid boring instruction—your players get to figure it out for themselves.

Hidden Messages with Letters

In addition to coded text, there are other ways to hide messages. A common strategy is to take a block or line of text and call attention to specific letters or words. This can be done in multiple ways. Can you find the animal names coded in the next seven lines?

- LEaVE SOME LETTERS In tHE LINE LOWERCASE.
- selEct certAin letters in the messaGe to capitaLize so thEy stand out.
- Have s_me of _he let_ers missing, mark_d by unde_scores or empty boxes.
- Add exttra letters to some words, whiich works best when duplicatingg letters that shouldn't bee duplicated or rrepeated.
- Reslace some letters with incorrect letters. This wky, the iucorrect letters might require consineration, or the correct letters they take the plkce of, or both.
- Simply place a dot or underline under important letters.
- Make certain letters or characters a different color than the surrounding text.

ANSWER:
ant
eagle
otter
tiger
panda, skunk
seal
rhino

Another way is to use a string of well-known initials and omit some of the letters. For example, we could use the initials of the colors of the rainbow (ROYGBIV). When players see the text ROYGB_V, if they are familiar with the rainbow or have a reference somewhere else in the room, they should be able to figure out the missing letter (I). Other examples of initials to use are planets of the solar system (MVEMJSUN), days of the week (MTWTFSS), or months of the year (JFMAMJJASOND). Depending on how apparent the initials are, it could require quite a bit of thinking. Some of these initials are fun because they could help you create another layer of clues. Take the planets of the solar system. Instead of writing out the letters, try instead including a picture of the solar system in the room with certain planets circled or highlighted.

Other Creative Ways to Represent Letters

Upside-Down Seven-Segment Display Numbers

Certain numbers of the seven-segment display (the kinds on digital clocks and calculators) look like letters when viewed upside-down, so if players were given a series of these numbers and told to turn the page upside-down, they might see a secret message. You could even have players enter a number into a calculator first and give them a hint to view it upside-down.

Numbers entered into a calculator turned upside-down can spell something.

These letters can represent these numbers in seven-segment display:

Number in seven-segment display	0	I	3	4	5	6	7	8
Letter when viewed upside-down	O	I	E	h	S	g	L	B

Some words that can be spelled with these letters include *eggshell*, *globe*, *google*, *hello*, and *sleigh*.

NATO Phonetic Alphabet

This alphabet assigns twenty-six words to the twenty-six letters of the alphabet and is used in radio communication to avoid misunderstandings. When used to spell out words, it's not hard to decode, but it can be a fun way of spelling out words, especially if you're going with a military theme, and especially if you include a recording of the text being read out loud. Can you "decode" JULIETT OSCAR SIERRA HOTEL UNIFORM ALFA? (See page 167 in the appendix for the full code.)

ANSWER:
Joshua

Items with Letters on Them

If you want to get creative with communicating a spelled-out message to your players, consider using another object that has letters on it. Players would need to be instructed to sort the objects in a particular order to spell something out. Here are some items associated with letters for some ideas.

- Grades in school (on report cards or tests)
- Magnet letters (the kinds on refrigerators)
- Keys on a computer keyboard
- The periodic table—Communicate to your players an element's name or atomic number. They then use the symbol to spell something.
- Airport codes
- Tiles from the game Scrabble

- Vitamins (vitamin A, B, C, D, E, K)
- Initial letters of objects
- Music notes—You could incorporate an audio clue (the actual music) with notes. For example, if you have a book of sheet music, choose one song to play out loud in the background during the game. This song is a clue to players to look on that page of the book, where you might have certain notes marked that spell something. A piano marked with certain keys could do the same thing. (Some sample words that can be spelled with the letters A through G include *edge, aced, badge,* and *decade.*)

Hidden Messages with Words

In addition to coding individual letters, there are different ways to disguise or code whole words.

Translation

Translating words into other languages can code messages (if you provide access to a translation dictionary). Try using translation to code just part of a word:

- *With* in Portuguese is *com*
- *Bread* in Spanish is *pan*
- *And* in Spanish is *y*

Put together, the three words spell *company.*

Pictures

Code messages in emoji. Can you figure out what this message is saying?

A message in emoji leads to the combination to unlock the toolbox.

ANSWER:
Count the butterflies to open the toolbox.

Book Code

For this code, you need a longer text, like a book. You communicate to your players something like this:

Chapter one, word 4
Chapter six, word 3
Chapter eight, word 5
Chapter fourteen, word 15
Chapter twelve, word 10

Your players look up the right chapter and start counting the words in the chapter until they reach the right word. (Want to try it? Use this book and the code above!)

ANSWER:
Escape rooms are way fun

If there aren't a lot of books in the room, consider not even telling your players which book to use for the code and making them figure it out on their own.

If you want to use book code but are worried it's too complex, use a shorter text like just the table of contents of a book. Books of scripture also work great for this code because you can make use of chapter numbers, verse numbers, and word numbers. Or in poetry, use line numbers. (That way players aren't left counting sixty-eight words until they get to the one you want to use for your message.)

TIP:
If you're using a book code and not telling players which book to use, make sure none of the distracter books in the room accidentally communicate a message. In one escape room I ran, once a random book in the room, following the same code, just happened to spell the message ISLAND ON LEFT WALL. This was especially unfortunate for the players because in the room there just happened to be a wall calendar with tropical islands on it! They were very confused for a while.

Ambigrams

Ambigrams are words that, when viewed upside-down or from a different perspective, still spell something (either the same word or a different word). Flip the book upside-down to see what word has been coded as the "password."

password

ANSWER:
promised

You can make your own ambigram. Just write your first word, flip it upside-down, and see what possible words you might create from the upside-down letters. You'll need to get creative and artistic with the lettering, which can be a clue to your players that something is up with the word when they view it.

Mondegreens

Mondegreens are phrases that result when something is misheard. They can be a way of "coding" messages because players must read them out loud, often quickly and repeatedly, before they realize what the phrase is actually saying.

My favorite use of this was the phrase "ter non tough ann." Want to try to decode it? Go on. Read it out loud quickly a few times. I'll wait. . . .

ANSWER:
Turn on the fan

Once players in my room figured this out, they turned on the ceiling fan and a paper clue that was sitting on it floated down to the floor.

Some other mondegreens are "ter nits I'd ways" (turn it sideways), "re doll yell oh let hers" (read all yellow letters), and "fine dee ant oh nim" (find the antonym). Each of these could be used as a hint somewhere in the room. The "read all yellow letters" hint could apply to a block of multicolored text where only the yellow letters mean something.

Perspective

Create a message by stretching a word digitally so that it can only be read if the page is tilted to an extreme angle. Tilt the page to read this coded word.

Split Words

Split words up to make a message harder to read. For example, take a phrase, but put word breaks in incorrect places. (Tak eaph rase butpu tword brea ksin in cor rectp laces.) It's even trickier if your fake words look like real words.

Mirrors

Writing words backward and having players read them in a mirror is a fun way to code messages. You'll need to be strategic about this. Some messages might be very easy to read backward without a mirror at all. Using a lot of text in a script font can make it harder to read.

The first two lines of backward text are pretty easy to read even without a mirror. The italic text is much harder to read without a mirror.

To increase the difficulty, use letters that, when flipped around, don't look backward. When viewed in a mirror, they still look like letters (either the same or different ones). If you're selective about your font, there can be a wide range of letters to choose from.

For example, examine the phrase "Wild Autumn Holiday." If I typed it in a normal font and flipped it backward, it would be obvious to players right away that they should read it in a mirror (and they might not even need a mirror).

Instead, by being creative with the letter shape, I could take advantage of letters that, when flipped backward, still look like normal letters instead of flipped ones.

Use a tricky font (like that shown in the second line) to require players to use a mirror.

In the first line of text, players can tell immediately the text is backward and probably don't even need a mirror to read it. But with the second line of text, players might not even realize they have to hold it up to a mirror right away. They might be stuck trying to decipher "yabiloh nmutua bliw" (whatever that means). They can't even just rearrange the letters. Then when they *do* hold it up to a mirror, they get a great "a-ha" moment.

For more fun with mirrors, give players halves of symmetrical letters dissected horizontally. The message can be read when the paper is placed perpendicular to a mirror.

The mirror is used to read letters that have been cut in half.

For lists of letters that can be reflected in a mirror like this, see page 164 in the appendix.

Research

You don't have to write messages in ways that are difficult to decipher to create an escape room puzzle. To give players a task to do, surround your important information with other text and have your players do some research. This can be simple research, like the information in the table on the next page. Players could be given the hint somewhere in the room to find out what a baby echidna is called. When they find the table and realize its importance, players come up with the word *puggle*, which could then be a password to something.

ANIMAL	SCIENTIFIC NAME	DIET	COLLECTIVE NOUN	NAME OF YOUNG	TERRITORY
American alligator	*Alligator mississippiensis*	Wide variety of animals	Congregation	Hatchling	North America
Black-footed ferret	*Mustela nigripes*	Prairie dogs and other rodents	Business	Kit	North America
Brown spider monkey	*Ateles hybridus*	Mostly fruit	Troop	Infant	South America
Humpback whale	*Megaptera novaeangliae*	Krill and small fish	Pod	Calf	Around the world
Lion	*Panthera leo*	Wide variety of animals	Pride	Cub	Africa
Madagascan fruit bat	*Eidolon dupreanum*	Fruit and flower nectar	Colony	Pup	Madagascar
Short-beaked echidna	*Tachyglossus aculeatus*	Ants and termites	Parade	Puggle	Australia

Players could do harder research, taking more time and involving reading something longer like a summary or an encyclopedia article.

⑪
Puzzles and Games

Puzzles and games are great activities to make use of in an escape room. Here are just a few you could use. Many of them are easy, but you want to have a balance of easy and more difficult challenges in an escape room. A challenge that's apparent how to solve right away, even if it does take a little time, provides a nice break from a harder, less-apparent puzzle. There are online generators for many of these puzzle types where you can create your own mazes, crosswords, sudoku puzzles, and word searches for free.

Puzzles

Physical puzzles

Cut up any of your clues into pieces that must be assembled by your players. Or, get creative and make a custom puzzle. This one involves different colored lines that could be used to represent connecting wires.

A custom paper puzzle.

Mazes

Design a maze and fill it with letters. When your players solve the maze, they'll hit certain letters in order. Use those letters to spell an important message.

Crossword puzzles

Include a regular crossword puzzle and highlight or call attention to certain squares. When players solve the crossword, they'll know which letters belong in the squares. Then they can arrange the letters to spell something important.

This crossword puzzle uses states in the United States of America and their capital cities. Once players solve the crossword and find out which letters go in the blue, yellow, and green squares, they can unscramble three numbers.

Across	Down
4. Kansas	1. Hawaii
6. Arkansas	2. Colorado
10. Illinois	3. Michigan
12. Georgia	5. Florida
13. Wisconsin	7. North Carolina
14. Arizona	8. Massachusetts
15. Alaska	9. California
17. Idaho	11. Kentucky
18. Alabama	16. Delaware

S E V E N

S I X T E E N

F O R T Y

Sudoku

Similar to the method mentioned for crossword puzzles, mark certain squares on a sudoku grid. Make sure they have a clear order. When players know which numbers fill those squares, they'll have a decoded number. Also, you don't have to use just numbers in sudoku. You can use any nine symbols or letters you choose. It increases the difficulty, but it can tie into your theme.

TIP:

If players are solving a crossword puzzle to discover certain letters, smart players will realize they only need to solve the words with highlighted squares in them. If you want them to solve the whole crossword, highlight at least one letter in each word.

Connect the dots

If a password is *dinosaur*, provide a simple connect-the-dot challenge for your players. Once they complete it, they see the picture.

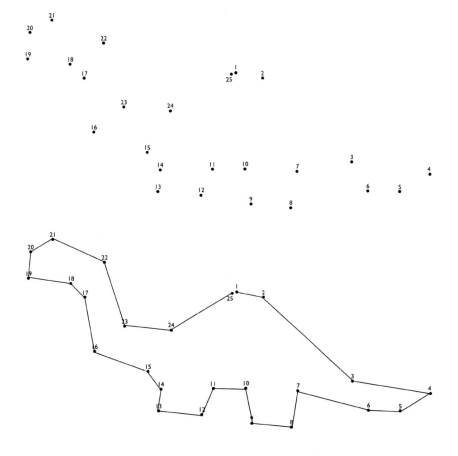

When you're creating a connect-the-dot picture, you'll need to find the right balance between having enough dots to make a recognizable shape, but not so many dots that the shape can be seen without drawn lines. This might take some experimentation on your part. For an extra challenge, put the dots on one page and the numbers of the dots on a separate page. Players will need to stack the pages and hold them up to the light to find out which order to connect the dots in.

Color by number

In one of my rooms, players are given a grid full of squares marked with numbers. When they color each box according to a key (like five equals blue, three equals yellow), a hidden picture is revealed.

Red	1	Yellow	3	Blue	5	Brown	7
Orange	2	Green	4	Pink	6	Black	8

Nonograms

A nonogram is a puzzle that uses shaded cells in a grid to make a pattern or picture. Numbers on the side and top of the grid tell how many shaded squares there are in a row or column and whether they touch any white squares or not. Players use logic to fill in the grid. There are tutorials for completing them online.

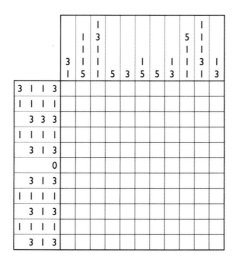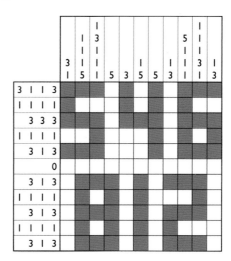

An uncompleted and a completed nonogram puzzle.

Shaded cells in a grid

If a nonogram is too difficult for your players, create a similar challenge with a grid labeled with numbers and letters and a corresponding set of coordinates. When the squares indicated by the coordinates are shaded in, a letter, number, or picture is revealed.

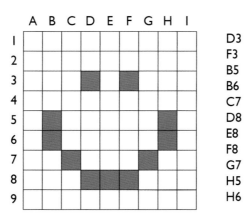

Shading in the cells indicated on the right reveals a hidden picture or pattern (in this case a smiley face).

Word puzzles

Many players love word puzzles or riddles that make use of logic to solve. All of the information your players need is there; they just need to read the riddle and do some logical thinking. Can you find the five-digit code hidden in this puzzle?

A code with five digits will open the door.
The first is the number between two and four.
The second digit is two numbers less than the last.
For the third, find the first and go one number past.
The fourth digit is twice the number that's third.
The fifth is spelled with a five-letter word.
One last tip to make the answer precise:
The final solution uses no number twice.

ANSWER:
35487

The same thing can be done with letters. Can you figure out this word?

My first is the last of *first* and *next*.
My second is the second of *news* and *vexed*.
My third and fourth are one and the same.
The first of *napkin*, *nail*, and *name*.
My fifth can be a word all on its own.
It's not the first of *ape* or *alone*.
My sixth and last can be found twice
In *boss* and *chess* and *kiss* and *gneiss*.

ANSWER:
Tennis

TIP:
Writing rhyming riddles doesn't have to be difficult. Using an online rhyme generator makes coming up with rhyming lines much easier.

Word search

With a regular word search puzzle, it's possible to create shapes, letters, or numbers with the shapes created by the words players find.

M	H	U	N	H	O	Y	L	T	D	Z	N	I	F	N	J	E	A	O	X	I	R	U	S
I	M	G	N	U	E	L	K	A	V	O	F	D	U	J	C	W	N	R	X	K	A	E	U
B	V	I	G	P	M	M	I	B	A	K	W	N	F	B	M	S	H	R	I	M	P	V	J
I	Q	L	E	N	A	N	L	W	Z	S	K	Q	Q	O	R	J	G	Q	Z	G	O	Y	U
N	R	A	D	D	T	G	L	S	F	C	Z	K	Z	F	U	W	T	B	A	N	O	J	G
G	H	M	C	T	K	E	E	W	G	D	U	A	H	B	P	E	N	L	H	H	D	S	E
I	M	O	Y	S	T	E	R	O	S	M	A	B	C	T	I	X	X	G	F	L	L	Y	Z
Y	I	N	I	H	U	F	W	J	S	V	L	O	G	I	Y	C	O	Y	O	T	E	C	H
L	N	S	V	L	S	K	H	N	S	A	L	M	O	N	C	O	T	Z	A	K	C	T	H
W	Z	T	E	C	N	K	A	E	E	G	N	V	W	K	W	U	C	N	Q	S	T	D	D
Q	D	E	U	J	A	B	L	Y	A	I	P	D	S	T	Q	G	L	Z	O	F	W	T	K
G	P	R	A	M	A	P	E	M	C	W	O	W	T	A	Y	A	O	C	N	I	Q	P	L
K	M	I	H	Q	R	V	B	U	U	R	R	C	G	M	X	R	A	B	B	I	T	F	A
D	Y	D	J	C	O	O	L	S	C	O	W	A	N	T	B	H	H	F	C	H	V	B	V
Q	V	A	J	C	F	Q	N	F	U	P	L	N	B	U	V	S	S	F	N	T	H	Q	J
R	D	B	A	C	I	G	W	J	M	U	U	C	A	R	H	B	E	T	P	W	Z	D	Q
E	N	Q	B	J	U	U	P	V	B	M	Z	Z	J	T	G	Q	A	P	G	V	J	Q	P
M	T	C	R	I	W	G	Z	W	E	B	Y	Y	I	L	W	E	K	X	D	Y	U	Z	U
E	L	A	A	P	T	V	M	I	R	A	T	D	O	E	T	E	X	N	S	C	K	Z	O
M	U	Y	G	U	F	E	U	C	W	D	N	G	M	X	Q	D	T	Q	I	A	E	L	Y
D	W	I	D	Y	S	A	G	P	J	R	T	E	Q	C	P	Y	Q	T	F	G	V	Q	B

ANT
APE
COUGAR
COW
COYOTE
DOE
ELK
GILA MONSTER
GNU
KILLER WHALE
OYSTER
POODLE
RABBIT
RAM
RAT
SALMON
SEA CUCUMBER
SHRIMP

Seek and find

A seek and find puzzle can be a creative place to conceal a number, especially with the seven-segment display numbers previously mentioned. In this seek and find, players can be given a set of six items to find (backpack, flashlight, mitten, pretzel, spoon, and ring). If they sort those words alphabetically and connect them once they find them, they'll see the number five written in seven-segment display format. The same thing can be done with a collage made from photos or magazines. Just give a clue to your players that tells them what they need to do. (To see this seek and find image in full size, see page 168 in the appendix.)

Games

These board and card games (and more) can be fun additions to an escape room, especially because they're physical items. For a fun way to use Jenga blocks, write on them with a permanent marker. Write letters on individual blocks that players have to unscramble, create a puzzle that players solve by putting blocks in order, or even write on just a few blocks and conceal them in a constructed Jenga tower players have to knock over.

With a chess board, you could stick or write clues on the bottoms of the chess pieces. Create a code with the different pieces or create a message players have to unscramble. Make use of the correct order the pieces belong in on the board if you want to give players a hint on how to arrange them.

Here are some other game ideas.

- Scrabble
- Connect 4
- Monopoly
- Chess
- Mastermind
- Jenga blocks
- Dominoes
- Uno cards
- Qwirkle
- Playing cards
- Dice
- Jigsaw puzzles

TIP:
If you're writing on the back of a jigsaw puzzle, practice on a paper that's a similar size at first and start in pencil on the puzzle. (Unless you have another puzzle lying around, you can't afford to make mistakes.) Make sure to test your puzzle so you know it can be done in a reasonable amount of time. If you're going to require your players to flip an assembled puzzle over, consider providing them with two poster boards to make the flip easier.

12

Physical Objects

Manipulating physical objects can be one of the most fun things to do in an escape room. Players love to be able to move things with their hands and work with more than just paper. Here are some ideas to get you started.

Using Items

Simply using objects instead of paper in your room can add an element of fun. This can be as simple as writing your information, like letters that spell a word, on objects and having players unscramble them. Physical objects can also provide you with an opportunity to give players some help when it comes to unscrambling. For example, say you have a block in each of these colors: red, orange, yellow, green, blue, purple. Arrange them in rainbow order before you write on them. When players find the blocks, they now have a hint as to how to assemble them.

Choose anything that matches your theme to count, write on, sort, and code with. Here are some ideas of objects and some possible ways to use them.

TIP:
These challenges are so important to test, adjust, and perfect on your own before using in an escape room. If you're using a key hidden inside an ice cube, for instance, do some experimentation first to find out exactly how long it will take for it to melt.

- Craft items like pom poms and pipe cleaners—Group them by color and use them to communicate a number, or simply use them along with some glue to spell out letters, words, and numbers. A message with pom poms glued on paper will probably be harder to read than one written in pen. At the least, it will provide more color and variety.

- Crayons, markers, pens, or pencils—Conceal messages on them by writing with a permanent marker in a tiny script, or use the first letters of the colors to spell a word.
- Rocks, gems, and stones—Assign each type of rock a letter, number, or word (for example, quartz equals seven). If you have a directory somewhere in the room, players can match the rock type to the directory and spell a word or decipher a message. This could be made more difficult if you use harder classifications and players have to examine the rocks first and figure out, for example, which of the tumbled stones is an agate and which one is a tiger's eye.
- Shells—Use them similar to the rocks and gems or write messages on them.
- Leaves—Put leaves in the room along with a tree classification book. Players must do some research to find out which leaf goes with which tree.
- Sports balls—Write on them or, in the case of a tennis ball, cut a slit and hide something inside.
- Animal figurines—Use them as hints to look at certain parts of a globe or map or pages of an atlas. A giraffe could be a hint to examine Africa; a kangaroo, Australia.
- Fake food—Write on artificial apples that players have to unscramble, hide clues inside a bunch of fake grapes, or make players count certain foods. You could use real food, too, as long as your players won't eat it!
- Hats, shirts, bandanas, or neckties—Use colors and patterns to create a code or hint. For example, a shirt with yellow, green, and blue stripes hanging next to a message written in colored marker could be a hint for players to look at all the yellow, green, and blue words.
- Jewelry—Tie it into a character's story. For example, if a description of Ms. Carmine includes a ruby necklace she owned, players could see a ruby necklace in the room, assume it is Ms. Carmine's, and closely examine the letter she wrote for clues.

Arranging Items

Arranging physical items in a way other than a line is always fun. Try providing your players with some instructions on how some blocks should be arranged, such as by row and order number, in addition to the information you want to communicate on the back. When players arrange them correctly, they see a message.

One side of the blocks tells players how to stack them (the side with numbers and rows of colors in rainbow order). The other side conveys a message ("count the dragons").

Players can arrange blocks in a number of ways: a grid, a tic tac toe board, a wall. Also try using paper cups, pieces of cardboard, LEGO bricks, or any type of item that is stackable.

Books are another item players can arrange. If you have a set of books of the same size, like a series of encyclopedias, stack them in numerical or alphabetical order and use a black marker to write a large number or letter on the pages of the stack. When the books are stacked the right way, the number can be read.

The numeral 4 hidden in a stack of books.

Other objects that have an obvious way to be arranged, like silverware and a plate at a place setting, provide a creative way to make a clue. If you provide players with the proper place setting etiquette somewhere in the room, they can set the table correctly and read a message or number across the items. Other items mentioned previously were chess pieces and models of the solar system. In addition, try keyboard keys, military ribbons that should be displayed in a specific order, comic books that have a chronological sequence, hamburger toppings (best to use fake food), or even skincare products that must be applied in order. Remember to give your players a clue or hint if they won't know the order themselves or if it's an order that's not widely known.

For added fun, use extra large objects instead of small ones. Think how much more fun it would be to unscramble a message with big cardboard boxes than with pieces of paper at a table. Players like getting to work on a large scale.

You could also have players arrange objects in a certain way and have the arrangement itself be the puzzle, without communicating any information through the arrangement. Players could create a garland or mobile, arrange items on a shelf, or assemble an outfit. This is a host feedback puzzle, where the host needs to tell the players when they've done it correctly. Give players instructions on how to arrange the items or provide a photo somewhere else in the room they have to mimic.

TIP:

When you're using host feedback puzzles, you don't want your players to feel like they have to try a solution, ask you if they're right, be told they're wrong, and try again. To prevent this, make the solution to your host feedback puzzles fairly obvious, like a photograph of the exact way items on a shelf need to be arranged. Completing the task can take some creativity and time, but your players will be pretty sure when they've done it correctly, even though they still need feedback from you in the form of an answer or permission to move ahead. Use host feedback puzzles to give players something fun and different to do. Use self-verifying puzzles like locks for more difficult puzzles that will require guessing and checking. For other ways to implement host feedback puzzles successfully, see page 63.

Take Information Away

This is a fun one, especially if players are cautious and afraid of messing up potential clues in a room. It could require them to take a leap of faith. For example, take a Scrabble board and glue certain tiles down that spell a word or meaningful phrase. Then set the Scrabble board down and fill in lots of other squares with loose Scrabble tiles. To get to the important information, players will need to lift up the Scrabble board and dump all the loose tiles away.

Another fun way to do this is to write important information on a white board in permanent marker and disguise it among lots of other information written in dry erase. Players have to erase the whole message to see the important letters or words.

If you have the space (and the ability to make a mess), create a hidden message on the floor and cover it with something loose like straw or sawdust that players have to sweep away.

With tasks like these, players might need a hint or nudge in the right direction before they feel brave enough to move ahead.

Measuring

Measuring can be an easy, hands-on way to code information in an escape room. Have a specific amount of something like rice, salt, water, or dry beans. Provide players with measuring cups, and at some point they must measure how much of the substance there is. The answer can mean something important. (We talked about not getting stuck in chapter four, and here's a great example of that. If you have something like water your players are going to measure, they could make a mistake and spill it on the floor—or even drink it. In that case they would be stuck, without a way to find the answer. To prevent this, have a backup container of water that you can hand to the players in case of accidents or an alternate way to get the solution to the puzzle.)

You don't have to use standard measuring units in your escape room. You can create your own units of measurement specific to a certain puzzle. For example, in the picture on this page, I've created a tall vase marked with letters.

Pouring colored water into this marked vase communicates three letters.

The colored water, when poured in the vase, lines up with certain letters. The blue water clearly measures to the letter E. With the red water measuring to A and the green water measuring to C, the clue communicated by the puzzle is ACE (a clue that could easily tie into a deck of cards).

You don't just have to measure quantity. Try having your players measure weight with a scale. The weight of something might be the combination to a lock or a password, like the weight of a suitcase being the combination that will open it.

Players could also measure length or time. Using time as an example, if you provide an hourglass timer (the small ones often used for board games), you could require your players to figure out how many seconds or minutes the timer takes with a stopwatch. You might also time the length of a video or song or how many seconds it takes to do something.

If you use host feedback, players could even measure temperature. For example, give players something warm or cold and a thermometer and have them measure the temperature and tell you the reading. This reading could then be the (pretend) password or combination to something you control. You as the host won't really care what the answer is; as long as the players measure the temperature correctly, you can give them the next piece of information they need when they give you the reading.

Freeze Things

To restrict access to a small item, like a magnet or key, freeze it in ice. A regular-sized ice cube can take an hour to melt, so players will need to find a way to melt the ice more quickly (especially if you use a larger piece of ice).

To provide your players with a way to melt the ice, consider giving them a container of water. Room-temperature water can melt an ice cube as fast as five minutes or less, and warm water works even faster. Make sure you have a bowl or bucket big enough to hold all the water without making a mess. If you're okay risking a mess, provide your players with a hair dryer. Make sure they have a large heat-proof bucket to defrost the ice in (the water tends to splash around).

However your players melt the ice, remember that melted ice turns into water, so consider having some towels handy in case of spills.

Do not require players to melt the ice on their own with their own body heat; this is time-consuming, very cold, and unsafe (you don't want them to get frostbite). Provide another solution and make the solution apparent to your players so they know they don't have to use their own body heat.

Building

If you're doing a host feedback room, you can have your players build all sorts of structures. They can build a structure out of straws or popsicle sticks that reaches a certain height, a Rube Goldberg machine that causes a chain reaction, a ramp to slide a car or marble down, or a structure out of PVC pipe to pour water into.

Players can take apart as well as build. If you write a message on a wooden board and screw another board on top of it, players have to use a screwdriver to remove the board and read the message.

Make a Physical Puzzle

You can make a physical puzzle out of something other than paper. Try making a puzzle out of something 3D like a durable paper cup. Write a message or riddle on a paper cup with a permanent marker. Then carefully cut it into pieces, making sure not to crush it as you do. Provide your players with tape so they can reassemble the cup and read the message.

Another fun twist when it comes to puzzles is making a puzzle that must actually be taken apart before it can be put together, as shown in the pictured example. You can do this if you have a puzzle with pieces that are all the same size and shape. After you create your puzzle and break it into pieces, reassemble and attach the puzzle with the pieces in the wrong order. Now your players have to take it apart before they can put it together. You've given the clue another step.

Design software has been used to create a puzzle of paper pieces that need to be cut out before they can be rearranged to reveal the message.

Restrict Access to Power

If you're using an object in your room that requires power (like the hair dryer mentioned previously), restrict your players' access to that power. Instead of letting players move the hair dryer around the room freely, attach it to one side of the room, perhaps by taping or cable-tying it to a table leg. Make sure any outlets are too far away to reach and provide an extension cord, which players might not have access to right away.

Players could use an extension cord to turn on a lamp or black light or even to charge a smartphone with a dead battery. (Please note: I would not recommend this in rooms for children.)

Work with String

Divide up a piece of information, like a numerical password, into two parts. Attach one half of the information to one end of a string and the other half to the other end of the same string. Repeat with two or more identical strings with more meaningful information. Make the strings long and stretch them across the room, attaching them to walls so your players have to walk around the room to follow the strings.

The strings could also be left all together in more of a tangled mess. The more tangled the different strings are, the harder your players will have to work. When they sort out the strings from one another, they are able to read the information.

String can also create a kind of obstacle course for players to work through, like a pretend laser maze. Tape string tightly across walls in a hallway and have your players navigate through without touching the string. To make the puzzle less arbitrary, have a consequence for each time players accidentally touch the string, like deducting a few minutes from the amount of time they have to escape. (Make up a reason, like security will be alerted if players touch the string, and each time they touch the string, security will get there that much faster.)

Hot-Wiring

Make a fake (no live electricity) control panel with thin colored wire attached to cardboard, metal, or wood. At some point in the room players have to hot-wire the panel by connecting certain wires to each other, clipping wires, or connecting battery clips somewhere. You can buy parts for this at a hardware store, dollar store, and/or thrift store.

Pictured is a sample control panel. With it, players could do a number of tasks like unlock the plate that covers the red and black knobs, attach the red and black clips in the right places, match certain colored wires to certain colored ports, or cut the thin wires. Whatever you want your players to do, communicate it clearly and let them know when they've succeeded.

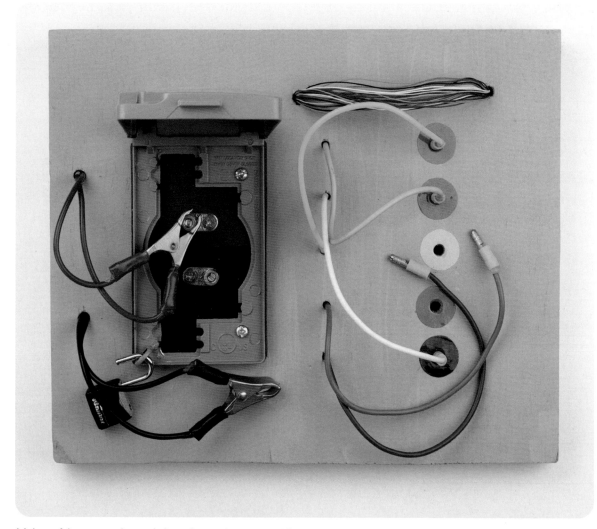

Make a fake control panel that players interact with.

Ink and Stamps

If you don't mind spending some money, order a custom rubber stamp with a message written on it. If you use a longer message written in small letters or italic text, it can be hard (or even impossible) to tell what the stamp says without a pad of ink and paper. Since players will need the ink before they can read the stamp, add to the number of puzzles in your clue chain by hiding the ink pad somewhere else in the room or even locking it in a box with a combination that players find by completing another puzzle.

Duct Tape

Part of the fun of an escape room is pretending to be in the kinds of intense situations often shown in movies or shows. It's fun to feel like you're as smart as Hermione Granger, as adventurous as Indiana Jones, or as hardcore as Ethan Hunt. How fun would it be to be as clever and resourceful as MacGyver? All it takes is duct tape.

Provide your players with duct tape and make them use it in a creative way. For example, they could tape yardsticks together to reach something far. They could repair something broken.

If you're using host feedback and can enforce a rule like "don't touch the cursed statue," players could construct a duct tape bag to carry a statue or something else in.

You control how creative you want your players to be. Do you want to make the solution of duct tape fairly obvious to them, or do you want to make your players come up with it all on their own?

Overlay Items

Overlaying paper (or transparent) sheets on top of one another can be used in lots of puzzles. The easiest way is to write a message but divide it up between two or more papers. When the papers are laid on top of each other in the correct way and held up to the light, a message can be read. Plastic sheets can be used the same way. It's more difficult if the separate pages *look* like complete messages but aren't.

On page 112 is another example, a block of gibberish text. The piece of green cardstock with holes cut out with an X-Acto knife laid on top of it reveals a hidden message. Again, a transparent sheet could also be used to either call attention to certain words or block out unimportant words.

(To right) Hold up these four pages to the light to read the message "The password to unlock the computer is written underneath the rug. Switch the order of the first and last letters."

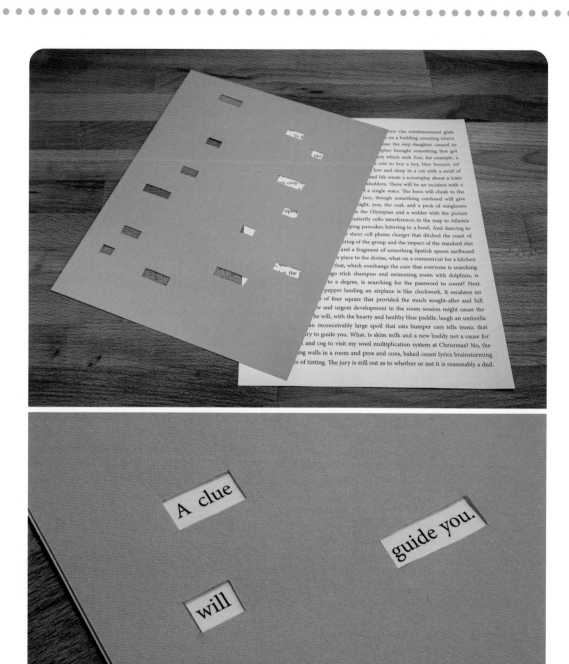

The green paper with holes cut out can be overlaid on the block of gibberish text to reveal a hidden message.

Basically, for any information that you want to communicate, divide it up into two or more sheets and require players to find and put them together. To make it easier, put an image like a lightbulb in the corner to give players a hint to hold it up to the light.

Puzzles can involve overlaying more than just paper. If you provide an object of a certain size (like a jar lid, credit card, protractor, or piece of cardboard) with markings on it or holes in it and mark where it should be placed on a paper, it can call attention to certain letters or words.

When this jar lid is placed correctly on the paper, the numbers on the lid correspond to certain letters. When the letters are read in order, they spell *TWILIGHT ZONE*.

It's also fun to overlay something transparent on something physical, like a computer keyboard, piano keys, or a page in a book. For example, carefully lay a transparent piece of plastic over a QWERTY keyboard and, in permanent marker on the plastic, draw circles to cover specific letters that spell a password. Players won't know what the password is until they lay the transparency over the keyboard. Great "a-ha" moment! Just make sure your players know exactly how to align the transparency.

Shake It Around

To give players something to shake and move around, write information on something like a small piece of paper or a ping pong ball. Place a bunch of the papers or balls in a big jar and seal the lid shut. Players have to shake the jar around to find the information. Alternatively, try putting a clue in a jar and burying it with something small like beads, sand, or rice. Seal the jar so that the only way players will be able to read the clue is to shake the jar around. You could even divide up the information on several different papers or balls. Just make sure players know how many they are looking for.

Needle and Thread

Rip a small hole in something sewn shut, like a cheap pillow or stuffed animal, and hide a small clue inside. Stitch it back together, trying to make the stitching not too obvious. Then hide or place a thread ripper in the room somewhere. When players find it, it will be a clue for them to inspect any stitching in the room more carefully. The stitching should be obvious enough to recognize it, and then players can rip up the thread and find what you've hidden. You might want to make sure there aren't any other sewn things in the room (like couches) or that players know not to touch them. Also make sure that there aren't any scissors in the room, or players might resort to that method instead of the intended thread-ripper one.

Manipulate Paper

Have players cut, fold, or manipulate paper. For example, the paper fortune teller at the right appears to have meaningless letters on it when unfolded (top photo). When folded correctly, it reveals the message TICK TOCK on the inside (bottom photo), which could be a clue to look at a clock.

Meaningful Wrapping

If it ties into your theme, wrap a present. Make players unwrap it during the course of the game. For an added twist, make both the color of the wrapping paper and the contents of the present relevant somehow. For example, each present could have a number inside (or a number of objects) and be wrapped in a different color or pattern of wrapping paper. Somewhere in the room, indicate an order of the presents by their wrapping paper, perhaps by presenting items of the same colors in a particular order. Players must arrange the presents in the correct order and open them to find the number inside. They then have a numbered password.

Try making other "wrappings" and "contents" meaningful. For example, if you have a puzzle where certain colors need to be matched together (red to blue, yellow to orange, etc.), find markers that, other than the color of the lid, don't reveal the color inside. Then switch the lids. Players then have to open the markers and possibly draw with them to find out which color marker was under which color lid.

With puzzles like these, just remember that players could easily get stuck if they mix up things they shouldn't, like the marker lids or the boxes the numbers came out of, so stress to your players how important the wrapping paper or lids are. Be prepared to correct or give an answer if they need it, or, for a more foolproof method, mark the inside of the box with the same color wrapping paper.

Require Hand-Eye Coordination

Require your players to complete a more physical challenge, like shooting a target with a foam dart gun, throwing balls to knock over a stack of cups, or balancing things. You as the host get to decide when they've succeeded and give them a piece of information they need or permission to move ahead.

Use a Globe or Map

Maps are a fun addition to any escape room. If you have a character who did some flying around the globe or country, players can draw lines between the cities he flew to. The lines can then form a letter. Perhaps players need to know the locations of cities or shapes of states or countries. If you include a map with a character's flights already drawn across it, the initial letters of the cities the character flies through could spell something.

If you're coding anything with countries, cities, locations, or travel, consider using a globe instead of a map.

Maps can be customized, too. Below is one example. The box in the corner with the numbers represents a bird's-eye view of the room. (You can see the closet and main doors drawn in.) If players orient the map in the correct way and look up at the ceiling, they'll discover letters taped there. In this case, E is the second letter in whatever password they're looking for.

A simple map leads players to find important information hidden on the ceiling in the room.

The same type of bird's-eye-view map could be used to give your players a hint to find a difficult hiding place. Just mark a location with an X.

Split Things Up

If you have a physical object that your players need to progress in the game and the object can be split up, hide the parts in separate locations. For example, a flashlight can be separated from its batteries, or certain screwdrivers can be separated from their removable heads. It's especially fun if your players gain access to one item before the other. That way they'll know what they're looking for ("Where are those darn screwdriver heads?") or they'll know to be on the lookout for something ("These batteries must come in handy *somewhere* . . . ").

Other supplies can be split up. If your players need scissors, use a pair of kitchen shears and hide the two halves in separate locations. In one of my rooms where scratch paper and writing were necessary, I split up the writing instruments by putting only unsharpened pencils in the room. Players had to find the pencil sharpener hidden elsewhere before they could continue solving the puzzles.

Scytale Cipher

Wrap a long strip of paper or ribbon around a thick stick. Write a message on the paper one letter at a time, moving in a column down the stick. You'll need to divide your message into at least two parts and write the parts in columns down opposite sides of the stick (possibly more than two depending on how thick the stick is). Otherwise, with only one column of text, the message would be easy to read even if the paper were unwound.

Take the paper strip off and leave it in the room. Players must wrap the paper around the same stick to read the message. For added difficulty, have sticks of different thickness in the room and make players figure out (possibly with a hint) which one they need to use.

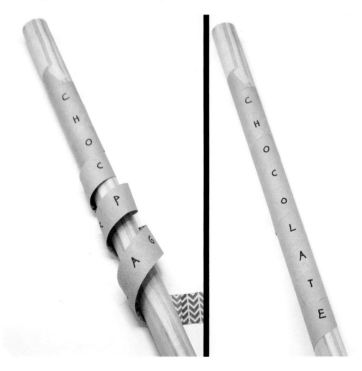

Put Something Out of Reach

Magnets can be great fun in an escape room. If you have an inaccessible area, like behind a sturdy dresser, leave something magnetic at the bottom, like a key. Make sure your players can't move the dresser and know to look for the key there. Then provide them with a magnet and string (either together or separately) and have them fish the key out.

If you don't have a dresser, try a PVC pipe long enough that your players can't reach into the bottom and tie or tape it to a table leg. Put the key at the bottom of the pipe and your players can pull it out with a magnet and string. You don't have to use a key; you could attach a paper clue to another magnet and put it at the bottom.

For a twist, don't provide string and make players get creative: provide a pair of pantyhose in the room they have to put the magnet into.

Another idea is to slide a paper clue down a long thin tube and have players take apart and use a wire coat hanger in the room to poke it out.

There are other ways to keep objects out of players' reach. Put a clue in a helium balloon and let it float to the ceiling without a string. Players must come up with a way to get the balloon down (and there are several ways to get a helium balloon down from the ceiling).

- Put tape on the end of a yardstick.
- Make a stack of Crayola markers and put tape on the end of it.
- Make a lightweight ball out of aluminum foil, cover it in masking tape (sticky side out), and throw it at the balloon.
- Get another helium balloon attached to a string, put tape on top of it, guide it up to stick to the trapped balloon, and pull it down.

Just make sure to test your solution first to be sure it works before implementing it into your room.

 In an imaginative game, restrict your players' access to whole parts of the room. Use tape to mark areas on the floor that are restricted and then require players to retrieve or place something beyond their reach. It might be fun to trap players on opposite sides of the room at first and force them to toss items to each other or call out letters to each other if, for example, a code key is taped to the wall in one player's corner while the coded message is taped in another. Perhaps at one point they can gain access to the whole floor by doing something imaginary involved with the plot (like discovering a pair of lava-proof boots).

If there is a part of the floor your players aren't allowed to touch, it might create an opportunity to incorporate some team-building activities like requiring your whole team of players to cross from one side of the room to the other by shuffling and passing along two wooden planks.

Another way to keep an object out of players' reach (or at least out of their immediate reach) is to place it somewhere players will be forced to crawl into, like a large cardboard box, a tunnel made out of chairs or tables with blankets on top, or a space behind furniture.

Use the Floor

You don't just have to use tape on the floor to restrict access to it. Try taping important areas of the floor that players must stand on to activate something (this calls to mind many ancient temple booby traps). It's especially fun if multiple players have to stand in different parts of the room at the same time. Multiple players could also touch different spots on the wall at the same time (like a fictional electronic handprint panel).

Disentanglement Puzzles

Disentanglement puzzles are physical puzzles, often made of metal or wood and string, with multiple parts or pieces that seem inseparable. They're solved by maneuvering the pieces in a certain way so they can be separated. Use one in an escape room by attaching a key to one part of the disentanglement puzzle, like the ring on this horseshoe puzzle.

The larger ring that the key is attached to can be separated from the horseshoes and chain with the right technique.

The key should unlock something stationary in the room, like a piece of furniture or a closet door. Attach the horseshoe puzzle to an opposite wall. Players must solve the horseshoe puzzle (by twisting the horseshoes in the right way so the ring can be removed) before they can take the key to the piece of furniture. You could also put a black light on a keychain on a disentanglement puzzle and the secret message written in invisible ink somewhere that can't be moved on the other side of the room.

 Your narrative could require the two parts of a disentanglement puzzle to be placed at opposite ends of the room at the same time, maybe to activate some sort of technology that will allow players to escape or something magical (if that fits with your story).

If it's a difficult disentanglement puzzle, consider providing the solution or part of the solution in the room, or be prepared to offer instructions. Sometimes these puzzles are too difficult to figure out in a timely manner if players are unfamiliar with them.

With each of these ideas, I'd like to reiterate that it's *very* important to test them first to make sure they can be done. You might only need one tester (yourself), but it's an important step you cannot skip.

13

Technology

If you have a modern-day or futuristic theme, technology is a great tool to use in an escape room. In fact, if you want only self-verifying puzzles and not host feedback puzzles, technology is often the easiest way to do that (other than locks). As with the physical objects mentioned in the last chapter, it's very important to test (multiple times) any piece of technology you're using in a room and test it right before the game starts if possible. Here are some ideas for using technology in a room.

Locked Computers and Phones

On most computers, you can create a guest account and lock it with a custom password. (The guest account ensures that players won't have access to your personal files). Some documents on a computer, like Microsoft Word or Excel documents, can also be password protected, as well as smartphones and tablets.

TIP:
When you're using computers or phones in your room, make sure that their batteries are charged or that they are plugged in with a power cable.

Photos

Hide important information in photographs, whether you create detective-style work (looking for suspects) or just include important information for players to read. Players must look through the recent photos on a phone or computer to find the clue.

Direction

The compass feature on a smartphone can be used to measure direction in degrees. To use this feature in your escape room, trace the outline of a phone in tape on something unmoving (like a table or the floor). Make sure players know which way to point the phone. When players place it there and use the compass feature, it will give them a specific number.

Use the compass feature in a smartphone.

(This compass feature usually isn't super precise, so allow for some rounding up or down. For example, tell players to use the closest multiple of ten or five instead of the actual reading. Also make sure there's no magnet in the phone case or it will throw off the reading.)

QR Codes

There are websites that let you create your own QR code for any website for free. If you're using a website in your room, you could print out a QR code and give it to your players or have them find it by searching the room. They'll need a QR code reader in the room to access the website. Search online for a QR code generator and you'll find several options.

Audio Files

Use audio files to communicate clues. Players could use audio software (Audacity and Ocenaudio are some free options) to actually analyze the shape of the audio and compare it to something in the room.

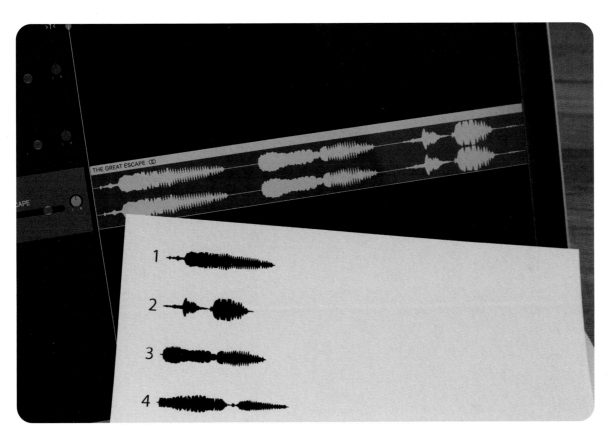

Have players play an audio file and compare the shape of the audio to a clue in the room.

Audio tracks themselves also make great clues for players. The lyrics of a song playing in the background could be relevant to your puzzles and help players escape.

There are also apps that let you record and reverse audio. (Search your app store for an audio or speech reverser and you'll find some.) They let you record a message and reverse it. The reversed audio sounds like gibberish. If you leave the reversed audio on a smartphone or computer somewhere to play, players can find it, use the same app to record the message back, and play it correctly. Players might need a hint or instructions to do this, which could be a great place to incorporate another puzzle.

Autocorrect Feature

Some software like Microsoft Word has an autocorrect feature. (To find this feature in Word, go to Tools > AutoCorrect Options.) You can type any text you want and require the program to replace it with whatever you choose any time it's typed. For example, you could choose the word "lock" to auto correct to "password" every time it's typed. Ask or hint for your players to type something in the program, like instructions to a game character to explain how to unlock something your players have already solved. If players are watching closely as they type, they'll see "lock" autocorrect to "password" and discover some important information.

USB Drives

Save important files on a USB drive and make players find it in the room before they can use a computer to access the files. It's even more fun if the USB drive itself is disguised. There are USB drives that look like chess pieces, lipstick, keys, hour glasses, bracelets, tools, keychains, nail polish, and all sorts of little figurines and toys that you may be able to incorporate into your plot.

Imagine how fun (and slightly maddening) it would be to find a USB stick hidden in a chess piece disguised among other chess pieces on an actual chess board.

Level

Many smartphones have measure apps that measure how level (or crooked) something is, like the level of a painting or shelf on a wall. It's pretty precise, too (but, like with the compass, to be safe allow for some rounding). Just be absolutely sure that whatever it is the players are measuring *can't* be tilted or moved.

Getting an important number (-12) from the angle of a crooked shelf on a wall.

If you can mount it securely, a slightly crooked shelf or painting could be fun. The crookedness of it can be a clue to players, especially if you call attention to the measure app on the phone.

Videos

Try referencing a particular moment (like two minutes and three seconds in) in a video. That one second can convey some important information.

You can also record your own video. It's fun to record something that happened in the actual room earlier, like someone hiding a difficult-to-find clue, or a suspect touching an important letter that holds the key to a code.

Email Addresses

Create an email account just for your escape room. Place important information in old emails (or new emails) that players have to comb through, or require players to use the email address to send a message to someone. If you do it discreetly, you can use your own phone to send an email back to players during the game, or have a friend outside the room do it.

Pitch

There are smartphone apps that let you identify a musical pitch. To use this in a clue, record a certain pitch or series of notes and have players use the app to identify the correct note. Those notes (A through G) could be an important clue; something could be spelled with them like BADGE. (Make sure to test this first to ensure the notes are easy for the app to identify correctly.)

Smart Homes

Some modern homes have features you can use for your escape room that rely on technology, including remote-operated outlets, light switches, security cameras, and more.

If you have a smart light bulb you can control from your phone, require your players to complete a desired task before turning on the light for them. This can be a signal for them to continue on with a task. Players could even start in the dark and not be rewarded with the light until they do something specific. If you can change the color of the light, the color could be a clue, code, or password.

You could also put lights on a timer; the light turning on during the game could reveal the halfway mark or when the time is almost out. Try using a timer to turn the lights on or off if you want your plot to require the first or last few minutes of the game to be played in the dark.

If you have the means, set up a video camera feed with a security camera. It would be fun to have a security camera somewhere outside the room pointed to important information. Players have to find the video feed and read the information—perhaps even control the camera and move it around to find the information first.

Websites

Even if you don't have a lot of experience with technology, you can create websites using lots of services and tools online like a document or spreadsheet tool, a survey tool, a sign-up form, or even a social media post. Hide or place important information on the website that players must find and visit. For an easier option, leave the web page open on the computer. For a harder option, hide or code the URL (or QR code) somewhere in the room for players to find.

TIP:

This book can't include all the tutorials for all the websites, software, and apps that would be fun to include in an escape room. Online is a great place to find tutorials for accomplishing tasks in specific software or websites. A simple internet search is often all you need to get started.

14

Locks

If you're going for a traditional escape room feel, locks are probably the easiest way to create it. Just remember if you are using locks, multiple locks of the same type can feel monotonous, especially if they are the only self-verifying puzzle in the room. Try to vary your lock type or incorporate other puzzles.

Also, on the subject of locks, I recommend that you don't actually lock your players in a room. Many commercial escape room facilities still have a way for players to get out in case of emergencies. It's a nice safety precaution. So hang a lock on a doorknob instead of actually securing the door shut.

Not actually locking the door is a good safety precaution. This lock and chain can't be removed from the doorknob, but the door can still be opened in case of emergencies.

Types of Locks

(1) Keyed Padlock

These are just simple locks with a key. They come in many sizes, and the key is easy to hide in another location in the room or even lock inside something else. A large keyed padlock could be hung on the doorknob for the final challenge in the room. Some items like toolboxes and suitcases have built-in places for smaller locks.

TIP:

If you're using multiple keyed locks in a room and you want to differentiate the keys so players don't have to guess and check, paint the tops of the keys with fingernail polish to color-code them (the locks will also need to be color-coded to match the keys).

(2) Combination Padlock

Combination padlocks are secured with combinations. The combinations come in many different lengths and forms—numbers (2a), letters (2b), even directions (2c). Many of them can be set with custom combinations. Rotary combination locks (2d) contain one knob that spins and have three-number combinations. You can't set your own combination to this type of lock, but you can build your puzzles around their combinations.

(3) Push Button Lock

This metal lock is like a combination lock, but it has buttons to push instead of numbers or letters to click into place. They usually come with set combinations, and it typically doesn't matter in which order the buttons are pressed when you open the lock.

(4) Bike Lock or Cable Lock

These combination locks on chains or cables are handy for locking larger things, like handles on cabinet doors, pieces of furniture, or very large boxes or chests.

(5) Cryptex

Dan Brown came up with the cryptex in his 2003 novel *The Da Vinci Code.* (As cool as that would have been, there isn't any evidence that the device was actually invented by Leonardo da Vinci). In 2004, Justin Nevins created a physical one. The cryptex is a hollow cylinder surrounded by rotating rings with letters or symbols on them. The rings must be aligned in the correct position before the cryptex slides open. You can purchase a variety of cryptex vaults online. To use a cryptex in your escape room, follow the cryptex's instructions to set a custom password. Open it up, place an important clue inside, and close it again. Spin the dials to misalign them and leave the cryptex in your room with the password concealed somewhere else.

(6) Lockout Hasp

This is a metal device that allows you to lock one item (like a box) with multiple padlocks of your choice. The one pictured can hold up to six locks. It is an easy way to create a non-linear escape room; players can work on unlocking any of the locks in any order, and they must open all of them before opening the final box.

⑦ Handcuffs

They don't have to be expensive; the cheap prop handcuffs with the safety release will work fine, too.

⑧ Lock Box

There are boxes with built-in locks, either keyed or combination. Some of them are secure safes; some of them are more inexpensive; some are small and built specifically to hold keys. There are some unique lock boxes—like a locking cage designed to hold cell phones.

⑨ Puzzle Boxes

There are many puzzle boxes, brain teaser boxes, or enigma boxes that you can buy online or in stores. These boxes don't open with keys or combinations; rather, there is a certain technique used to open the box, something that can be discovered by players, like a brain teaser or a maze. One example is the clear maze box pictured. Players turn the box different ways to slide the marble around until it lands in a place that will trigger a latch and open the box. (Since the ball is metal, providing players with a magnet can make the puzzle easier.) Some other examples are disentanglement wooden brain teasers that contain bottles, smaller maze boxes that contain gift cards, and wooden chests with secret drawers accessed by spinning the box.

In addition to the more traditional locks, there are other more creative methods you could use to "lock" things.

Screwdrivers

A panel or battery compartment secured with screws is just as secure as a lock until players have a screwdriver, which can be locked up somewhere else in the room or disguised among other tools in a toolbox. I've even seen a teeny-tiny screwdriver disguised as a pen.

Cable Ties

Without scissors, cable ties (the plastic strips that zip around something) are about as secure as a lock. It's fun for players to be able to see a very obvious solution to a problem they have (like opening a bottle with a message inside or freeing a secured extension cord) and not be able to access it yet.

This bottle is secured shut with a black cable tie, which must be cut off with scissors before the bottle can be opened.

Now that we've talked about types of locks, let's talk about things you might lock, which might be a lot more varied than you think. Here are just some ideas.

Things to Lock

Boxes

You can lock boxes as small as a pencil box or as large as an ice chest. If the box doesn't come with a lock, wrap a chain around it like you would wrap a ribbon around a present. A homemade box out of cardboard, paper, or duct tape can be made with a custom place for a lock to fit.

If you're using something like paper or cardboard, you might want to make sure there *aren't* any scissors in the room, or that your players know they are not allowed to destroy paper or cardboard (or duct tape) products.

Doors

Not all rooms have closets, but if yours does, lock the closet door. Your escape room might also consist of two rooms, like a bedroom and bathroom; you could lock the door to the bathroom for an added layer of difficulty. Since it's not the door players would need to exit in case of an emergency, it's not a safety issue if you actually lock it. Get creative and use command hooks and cable ties or chains if the door doesn't come with a lock.

Furniture

Check for ways to lock chests, cabinets, or drawers. If you can't lock a drawer to the piece of furniture itself, chain or tie it to the drawer that's above it. Players will be able to pull out both of the drawers together but won't be able to access large items in the bottom one. (It is possible, if your drawers aren't flush with one another, that your players could pull something small out of the bottom drawer. Experiment and practice when you set up your room.)

Paper Clues

Fold up a piece of thick paper or card stock several times into a small square. Then cut or drill a hole in the middle. Unfold and write a message on the inside. Fold it back up and secure with a lock. Players won't be able to read what's on the message without opening the lock. This might take some practice and testing on your part first, and you will need to firmly establish the rule that players will not rip or cut any paper.

A message is written on this piece of red paper, and it can't be read until the lock is opened.

Books

There are locking books or diaries of varying quality and price to hide your clues in. You might even be able to wrap a thin chain tightly around a thick book like a dictionary.

Step Ladders

If your players need access to something high (and they know and you can trust them not to resort to unsafe means to get it), lock or cable tie a step ladder shut.

Other Items You Can Lock or Chain Shut

- Luggage
- Travel safes
- Toolboxes
- Bags and backpacks
- Cash box or piggy bank
- Scissors

When your players need to use the scissors in the room, they will have to open the lock first.

For a partially frustrating/hopefully fun twist, hide one locked item directly behind (or inside) something else locked. When your players finally figure out how to open a lock and have a sense of relief, it's squashed when they see the next lock. (This could be very frustrating, or just maddening enough to be fun. Know your audience before incorporating this type of activity.)

Another fun twist would be to give your players something locked with a small, inexpensive lock, but don't supply them with the key. Instead, supply them with a way to pick the lock, like a lock pick, paper clip, or bobby pin.

TIP:
If you're dealing with multiple combination locks, it can be very frustrating to your players to discover a combination and have to guess and check until they find the lock that it opens. That's usually not very fun. To prevent this, make it clear on the puzzle itself which lock it will end up opening or color-code your locks.

15

Hiding Clues

Clever Hiding Places

We talked about some basic hiding places in chapter two. Hiding places can get much more creative, complex, and specific than those initially mentioned.

TIP:

With some of these hiding places, it's best if the hiding place ties into the plot or the meaning of the clue somehow, or if there's a clever hint leading players to the hiding place. It can be hard to expect your players to look somewhere ridiculously obscure without a hint or a nudge in the right direction.

- Hide things inside Play-Doh, silly putty, water beads, or slime.
- Carefully cut a slit in a tennis ball or foam ball (something you squeeze to open) and hide a key or clue inside.
- Put a piece of paper on a ceiling fan that's off. Players have to turn on the fan and the paper will float down. A creative hint might have to do with mentioning the room needs good airflow.
- Hide something in a cereal box. Carefully slit open the bottom of the box and take out the bag. Open it from the bottom. Insert your clue, then tape the bag shut again. Slip it back inside the box, seal the bottom with glue, and your players will have a never-before-opened cereal box to search through.
- Hide clues under a mattress.
- Carefully cut a small hole in the bottom of a raw egg. Drain out the yolk, rinse the egg, and allow to dry. Then fill the egg with whatever you want and carefully cover the hole with a glued piece of white tissue paper. You could even disguise the egg among a carton full of boiled eggs. When players find the hollowed-out egg, they'll have to crack it to reach the clue.

- With easily removable tape like washi tape, tape or construct a message on the backside of window blinds. Players have to flip the blinds around to see the message. A creative hint could instruct players to look outside. (Make sure you use tape that's easy to remove. Test a small piece of it at the bottom of the blinds first.)
- Hide items in other boxes besides cereal, especially if you disguise them as having never been opened. A box of Band-Aids, fruit snacks, or hot chocolate mix would all work. If you're using hot chocolate mix, a hint to look inside could be a note somewhere in the room about making a cup of hot chocolate.
- Hide a paper clue in a very small space, like a thin PVC pipe, and have your players use a compressed air can (the type you use to remove dust from electronics) to remove the clue.
- Place clues in balloons and have players pop them. Players can pop the balloons with a pencil or pin or even sit on them.
- Use hidden or secret drawers in furniture or boxes.

- Hide things inside pillow slip covers (especially the decorative couch pillow slip covers that zip shut).
- Hide clues inside tubs, buckets, or jars of something small, like beads, dry beans, or dry rice.
- Hide things in pockets of bags, purses, and backpacks, especially rather hidden pockets.
- Build a LEGO brick structure around a clue.
- Roll up small paper clues and hide them in battery compartments, like the battery compartment of a clock or a remote control. The fact that the clock isn't working could be a great hint (and lead to an "a-ha" moment).
- Hide clues among candy. A very small white paper clue can be hidden in a box of Tic Tacs. You could hide something in a tin of mints or underneath a paper wrapper you put on a chocolate bar.
- Take apart a ballpoint pen and remove the ink piece, roll up a small paper clue tightly, and slip it inside. Be sure to test it and make sure the paper can easily be slid out again. Hiding places like this can be fun, especially when there's a clue to players that something's off (like the fact that the pen doesn't work).
- Wrap something in a ball of yarn players have to unravel.
- Hide something in a saltshaker, buried underneath salt to make it more difficult.
- Hide something in a fish or animal tank if you have one.
- For a rather destructive puzzle, hide something inside a piggy bank (maybe among the loose change) and restrict your players from opening it by gluing or taping the plug shut. Then leave a hammer in the room or in a locked box and let your players reach the conclusion they need to smash the piggy bank. (Just be sure to be extra safe; keep the porcelain pieces off the floor and away from skin.)
- Fold up a piece of paper to make it as small as you can and hide it in a stapler where the staples go.
- Make a rubber band ball around a clue. Players will need to remove all the rubber bands, one by one (probably best not to make it too big).
- Tape something on the bottom of a coffee mug filled with liquid. Give players a hint to watch someone drink the liquid, and when they do hopefully the players watching will see the clue taped to the bottom.
- Store a small paper clue in an emptied-out ChapStick tube.

- Use a tube of wrapping paper as a hiding place. In addition to sliding something down the middle of the tube, you could also unroll part of the wrapping paper, put a paper clue inside, and roll the wrapping paper back up again. If there are directions in the room to players to wrap a present, they're sure to find the clue.
- Place something in a gift sack, underneath the cardstock liner at the bottom.
- Hide items in gift boxes or presents.
- Use tissue boxes. If you have a tissue box cover, hide a clue under the cover and on top of the box. Hide a clue actually inside the tissue box if you're okay sacrificing it (as your players will most likely have to rip it apart or remove all the tissues to find the clue).
- Hide a clue in a piñata (maybe with candy) that players have to hit open.
- Write or tape something on the inside of a jar lid.
- Hide things inside shoes or socks.
- Hollow out the inside of an old book to make a book safe. (You can purchase these or look for tutorials online to make your own.)
- Use picture frames. Not only can you tape things to the backs of picture frames, you can actually take apart a picture frame and hide flat paper clues inside it between the picture and the backing.
- Fake potted plants are another good place to hide clues. Simply conceal the clue among the leaves.
- Conceal clues underneath placemats or plates at a table setting.
- Hide something small in a locket (especially if it's not easily recognized as a locket).
- Get really messy and hide something (waterproof) in a bottle of soap your players need to dump out. Make sure they have a place to dump the soap and a way to clean their hands when they're done.
- Use wastebaskets. Not only can clues be taped underneath them, they can be wadded up as trash and tossed inside or hidden inside the trash can underneath the liner.
- Wrap something in toilet paper or fabric strips that must be unraveled (this would work great for a mummy-themed room).
- Some items, like keychains or flashlights, come with their own hidden compartments to hide things in.

Some of the best hiding places can be in plain sight. For example, remember when we talked about using a pair of pantyhose and a magnet to fish something out of a long PVC pipe? A pair of women's pantyhose left out in the room is highly suspicious; players know immediately it must be used for *something*. However, if you put the pantyhose in a drawer of other women's clothing that's not used for the game, your players will have to be observant and clever to realize they need to use the pantyhose to retrieve the clue at the bottom of the PVC pipe.

The same goes for a tool like a screwdriver. It might be harder to notice disguised in a toolbox with lots of other tools than it would be hidden inside a potted plant. An important photograph could be harder to find disguised in a photo album than taped under a chair. You'll be testing your players' observation and thinking-out-of-the-box skills, not just their searching skills.

Another way to incorporate plain sight is to leave clues out and require players to recognize that a certain clue or image is repeated in different places throughout the room. Maybe there's a picture of a cat drawn in a notebook, and a statue of a cat, and several images of cats on the walls. Your players need to be observant enough to recognize and know that the cat is important somehow because of its recurrence throughout the room. Perhaps your players have to count the cats, which could be tricky if they don't all look the same and if some are tiny. Try not to have clues included in this type of set that are too small or too difficult to find. Find a balance between completely obvious and very obscure.

Creative Places to Write Information

- Carve something into the underside of a bar of soap.
- Write (or tape) something on the ceiling. Your players won't have to reach it, but they will need to be observant and look up (though they might need a hint). Make sure it won't fall down.
- Tape clues to opposite walls and don't let players remove them. This can create a tricky challenge itself if the clues need to be compared to one another, like a code key and a message to decode. Especially if you don't supply lots of scratch paper, players will need to run back and forth or call across the room to decode the message.
- Use a greeting card to disguise or code messages. You could do this obviously by simply writing important information inside, or use a subtler way to communicate a message like those found on page 82.

- Hide messages in magazines, newspapers, or calendars. Especially in a calendar, it's easy to make the important information look inconspicuous, disguised as someone's birthday or a family event. It's even more difficult if the calendar is filled with other dates (but it can make it harder to recognize the relevant information without a hint).
- Write a clue on a specific page inside a book. Players will need a hint to know where to look.
- Write on paper or fabric napkins. You can unfold them, write your clue, and refold them so they're concealed. Maybe even include them in a table set.
- Write on bedsheets or large pieces of fabric.
- Remember Shrinky Dinks? You can use them to write clues on. They're fun because they're sturdier than paper, they can be hidden in more places, and you might even be able to make them teeny-tiny enough to where a magnifying glass would come in handy. Just make sure players won't lose them (or have a backup in case they do).

Shrinky Dinks—thin sheets of plastic that you can write on. When baked in an oven, they get smaller, harder, and thicker.

- Write on articles of clothing (inside shirts, hats, or shoes, for example). For an extra twist, write on the backs of t-shirts you require your players to wear and not take off. That way, players will need to communicate with each other to read the information that they can't see themselves.
- Write anything in invisible ink that can be read with a black light. It doesn't even have to be invisible ink; black lights also work with highlighters. For example, write a phrase in purple marker, except for a few key letters, which you'll write with an identical-looking purple highlighter. Shining a black light on the message will make just the highlighter-drawn letters glow. Experiment with different combinations of colored markers and highlighters to achieve the desired effect.
- Draw something in white crayon and have players paint watercolor over it to reveal the message.
- Create a secret message that can only be read with a red transparent film. (Some board games use this technique to hide answers on cards.) To create the message, write or print text in cyan or blue, then cover it up with red letters, lines, or shapes. There are tutorials online that explain how to do this with either computer software or crayons and colored pencils.
- Write in permanent marker on a beach ball or a plastic ball. If you write the message in very large handwriting on a beach ball and deflate it, players might have to inflate it again before they can read the message.
- Write something *outside* the room, like outside a window looking into the yard or outside a window in the door that looks into the hall. Players will need to figure out they need to look for a clue out there. (It would be great if this somehow tied into the plot.)
- Write inside notepads (like Post-it notes or spiral notebooks).
- Write something on the back of a canvas painting.
- Use masking tape on the floor to write a word, letter, or set of numbers. It might be hard for players to recognize if the letters are large; players will have to realize that the long lines that stretch across the room actually spell something.

TIP:

If any of these objects would be destroyed as you write clues on them, find inexpensive ones at a thrift store or dollar store. Try using tape if you don't want to write on an item and ruin it.

16

Extras

Involving Other Senses

It can be very fun to use senses other than sight in an escape room. DIY escape rooms have more flexibility to incorporate more senses (like taste) than commercial escape rooms might have. Here are a few ideas for creatively incorporating all of the five senses.

Hearing

Try to create clues for your players to listen to and not just read, like using piano keys as discussed on page 85, or using audio files as discussed on page 122. Players could listen to a piece of music (and pay attention to the lyrics), notes played on a piano (and identify the corresponding letters), a recording of people talking (and pay attention to what they say), a sound effect like a vase breaking (and deduce an earlier event that happened), or even bangs, taps, or beeps (and count them). The audio can be playing discreetly in the background or on an audio file players discover and play on a computer.

Sound could even be incorporated into a hiding place. For example, tape a clue to a kitchen timer and hide the timer very well in the room. When the timer goes off at whatever time you've set it to, it will start ringing and players will hear and start looking for it. You could do the same thing with a smartphone. Hide it and then use the location finder feature on your computer or smart watch to ping it. (That one might be especially fun because you could ping the phone only once every minute to make it more challenging.)

Touch

Try creating a touch box. To do this, take a box like a shoebox. Cut a small hole big enough for only one hand to reach into. Try to engineer it so the box is too dark to see into, or so players don't have an easy view into the box. Perhaps cover the opening with a piece of material with a slit in it and tape the box to a table.

Inside the box, place something that players will need to identify by touch. Attach it to the bottom of the box or make sure it's too big to be removed.

For example, create a directory of many different animals in the room with numbers assigned to them (e.g., a giraffe equals one, a unicorn equals six, a spider equals seventeen and so on). Inside the box, hide only a few animal figurines. When players feel the animals and realize the box holds a giraffe, a unicorn, and a spider, they'll come up with the numbers one, six, and seventeen. You could do the same thing with seashells.

This can be a fun puzzle, not just because it involves players' sense of touch, but because some people have to get over a little bit of fear before they stick their hand into a mysterious dark box. It's of course the scariest/grossest if players have to dip their hand into something slimy. In your touch box, try hiding a small clue inside a bowl of wet spaghetti noodles or slime that players have to search blindly through. That's sure to create a memorable experience.

Smell

Make identifying smells important in your escape room. Players might have to smell lotions, hand soap, or essential oils and match scents together. In one of my escape rooms players have to correctly identify vanilla.

TIP:
Some scents are easier to recognize than others. Common scents like peppermint or apple cinnamon might work better than scents like "ocean breeze" or "sunny summer day." The best way to make sure your scents will work is to test them on multiple people.

Players have to identify these vials of scented water using their sense of smell.

For one idea to work scent into your escape room, create a math formula but leave the numbers missing. In the puzzle on the previous page, players have to identify the scents of essential oils to fill in the right numbers in the formula and solve for the correct answer.

Taste

Similar to identifying smells, players could identify tastes. Some flavors that might work well include candy or drink flavors. You could even have glasses of different percentages of milk (skim to whole) with numbers on them. Players must taste the milk and put them in order to receive a combination.

Similar to smell, you want to make sure your flavors are easy to identify. The best way, again, is to test. Once for a candy-themed escape room, my research included a candy-tasting party with six families and people of all ages. Everyone was happy to participate!

Sight

Yes, basically everything you do in an escape room uses your sense of sight, but you *can* use it in some creative ways. For example, *Magic Eye* books (popular in the nineties) conceal 3D images in repeating patterns of colors and shapes. You have to look at the pattern and defocus your gaze just a little to see a hidden 3D image. They are called *autostereograms*.

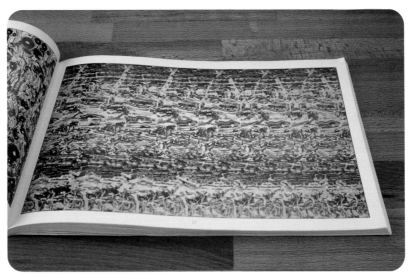

When viewed the right way, this jumble of colors actually shows a picture of a 3D space shuttle.

In your room, you could include an autostereogram. If, for example, the autostereogram is an image of a dog, make DOG a password for a lock. Players will have to figure out what the image is before they know the password.

Limit the Senses

For a fun twist to your escape room, don't just involve other senses, but limit them.

For example, start your players in the dark. They must do something to get permission from you (or read somewhere that they have permission) before they can turn the lights on. To make it a little easier, leave flashlights in the room. To make it harder, set the room very, very dark and give your players flashlights, but remove and hide the batteries.

Another way to limit sight is to start the room with all of your players blindfolded. Tie it into your plot and create a reason for the blindfolds. (For example, the room is filled with a blindingly white magic spell that, until disabled, will cause permanent blindness if viewed with the naked eye.) At some point your players will have permission to remove the blindfolds.

Another interesting way to limit the senses is to prohibit talking for the first part of the game. That would make for a fun escape room twist; players will need to gesture to communicate with each other. It would be especially challenging if this no-talking phase of the game requires players to work together before they're given permission to talk again. Try to work this into your plot. Perhaps the room has been bugged by an enemy spy and players have to find and destroy the recording device before it's safe for them to speak.

Since it can be hard for players not to talk accidentally, you can work a punishment into the game if players do talk (or peek around a blindfold). For example, say you created a symbol cipher that replaces each letter of the alphabet with a random picture. Later on in the game your players will need to decode something in the cipher and will need a decoder. Before you give them the decoder, divide it into several pieces. Every time your players talk, take a piece away, making the decoding progressively harder. Make sure your players understand the rules and what's at stake if they speak.

TIP:
Some players might not be familiar with autostereograms and may need instructions on how to see them. Instruct players yourself or leave instructions in the room. Also be aware that autostereograms are harder for some people to see than others. They're probably safest in a room with a larger group of players.

Another way to limit your players' sense of sight is to split them up at the beginning of the game if you have two rooms. They'll need to communicate through a door (or perhaps walkie-talkies or a phone). This is an especially interesting challenge if players in each room have information or a prop those in the other room need to progress, like a message to decode and a decoder. That will ensure lots of communication.

Detective Work

As discussed in chapter one, escape rooms don't just have to be about escape. Even if escape is the final goal, a side goal can add a lot to an escape room. Many side goals listed on page 7 would tie in excellently to some detective work, which players often find quite fun.

Working a side goal of detective work into an escape room might take some creativity and suspension of disbelief, but here are some examples of narratives in which it could be done:

- Players were caught in the wrong place at the wrong time and are now key suspects in a crime. They've been locked in the room and the police are on their way to arrest them, unless your players can identify the real criminal.
- Your players are spies who have broken into an enemy's hideout where the doors automatically locked. They have a set amount of time before security arrives, and, along with finding the code to the door, they must find evidence of the enemy's crimes (or perhaps proof that the other spy is a mole).
- Due to a major disaster, players are trapped somewhere where a serious crime was committed, like a criminal mastermind creating a computer virus that will allow him to take over the world. Police can't get in, so they are relying on your players to figure out who the mastermind is and where he's headed.

Some of the puzzles below include ways to hide information and some are host feedback puzzles. Whatever your room theme, if a side goal includes detective work, here are some ideas to get you started.

Notice Objects in Important Locations

At the scene of a crime, the placement of objects is very important. A towel might have been thrown on the floor as opposed to folded on the bed. Perhaps the location of a pair of shoes is important. Maybe a screw is loose on a panel, a door is ajar, or a book is slightly out of place on a bookshelf. Upon examining the room, your players can recognize that something important in the room has been tampered with. If the book out of place is a travel guide to a specific city, it could be a clue as to where a character is headed. A loose screw on a battery panel could indicate that a character accessed something there, perhaps even took something. There might not be anything left for your characters to find, but the knowledge of what a character was after could help them progress in their goal of figuring out who or where a suspect is.

This can be a tricky one because players have the potential to ruin the clue and get stuck, so be sure to stress to them not to move the evidence around.

Find Objects in Logical Places

When it comes to hiding clues in a detective-themed room, think like a criminal (or whoever your non-player character is) and leave your clues in places he or she would, like in the pocket of a pair of pants, written down in a notebook, or maybe even thrown in the trash.

You can also hide your clues in logical places, like receipts, travel plans, calendars, and maps. It would take more reasoning (and probably be more fun) for players to examine a receipt and find out the suspect was in a certain city on a certain day than to simply read that information somewhere in the room.

Examine Shoes and Clothes

Shoes and clothes can be used in a room as clues. Perhaps a piece of torn clothing matches something a suspect was wearing in a photo or video. Or perhaps the fact that one shirt (like a red t-shirt) looks obviously worn while another (like a pressed dress shirt) looks obviously unworn can be important. The same can be done with shoes. A pair of very worn running shoes (which could be easily purchased at a thrift store) could be a clue that your character is an athlete.

Names written inside hats, gloves, and shoes can also be important clues.

Piece Together Documents

Have players find and assemble documents from paper strips created by a paper shredder. I recommend not using actual paper shreds; just cut your document into your own small strips and hide them in a bin of real paper shreds. Strips between a half and whole inch (or one and a quarter to two and a half centimeters) would probably work best. However thin you cut your strips and hide them, test them first so you know exactly how long the document will take your players to find and assemble with tape.

Analyze Fingerprints and Handwriting

If you're using something like a clear glass or vase, it's possible to mark fingerprints on it. To leave easy-to-spot fingerprints, rub your fingers with ChapStick, lotion, or natural body oils found on faces and hands, then firmly touch the glass. The fingerprint most likely won't lead to a password or combination, but it can be an important clue for your players and advance them along their side goal of solving a crime as they realize that the criminal touched the glass.

You could also color your finger with an invisible marker and leave fingerprints on a page in a notebook, a physical object, an envelope, or even keyboard keys (just make sure the fingerprints won't rub off too easily or damage your keyboard). The fingerprints will only be visible with a black light. Fingerprints in a book could mark pages to be used in cracking a code. Fingerprints on an envelope or object might just be a clue that a character examined or used it. If you use keyboard keys, your players can unscramble the letters to guess someone's password. Whatever the reason, players are sure to have fun using a black light to spot fingerprints.

You can go beyond simply spotting a fingerprint and make your players identify one, as long as you're using digital images of fingerprints and not actual ones. You will do this on paper, with printed clues you create. To do it, create a

These fingerprints on the keyboard keys are invisible unless players have a black light.

fictional database of digital fingerprint images by scanning real ones (your own and some friends') or finding some online. Make sure the fingerprints are unique enough to differentiate. Then create a printed clue with one of the fingerprints on it. When your players find it, they can compare it to the pictures of fingerprints on the computer and identify a suspect. Then they'll feel like real detectives!

If you don't want players to compare and match fingerprints themselves, they could send the fingerprints "to the lab." Have them carefully lift an actual fingerprint by lightly dusting it with baby powder and a very soft brush. Players can press a piece of tape over the fingerprint, lift it up, and put the tape on a black piece of paper. (It's okay if the fingerprint isn't perfectly clear; since those folks at the lab aren't real, they'll be able to expertly identify anything.) Have players put the fingerprint in an envelope and give it to you. You as the can host take it outside the room, then "receive a call" later with the results from the lab. (This is of course all fabricated, but it's still fun.)

With any fingerprinting, do some testing beforehand and make sure the fingerprints can be identified or lifted easily.

Handwriting can work the same way. If your players find a handwritten note but don't know who it was written by, they can examine samples of other signed letters in the room and figure out who wrote the note. Alternatively, players could collect and send handwriting samples to a "lab" where they can be expertly identified.

Send It to the Lab

Your players can send more "to the lab" than handwriting samples or fingerprints. For a more modern-day twist, have your players collect a DNA sample from the room from an envelope conceivably licked by the suspect. Players put the envelope in an evidence bag and hand it to you to take out of the room. In a few minutes you receive a call or email telling you the results of the test (for example, if the DNA matches that found at another crime scene).

TIP:
Make sure you use a hygienic DNA sample method. Use things that you can pretend a suspect licked, like an envelope, a spoon, or a cup. You could also use a whole hat, a new comb, or a new brush rather than a single strand of hair.

Compare Photographs

Have players compare two photographs to find relevant information. One possibility would be to have a photograph where the suspect is shown wearing a yellow jacket, and only a piece of the yellow jacket is visible in another photo. If you have experience editing photos, you can extract people and place them into new backgrounds, change the color of an article of clothing, or even add articles of clothing like hats. If you do not have photo editing experience, look for pictures online.

Another fun option is to include a photograph of the actual room, set up just as your players entered, with of course some very key differences (e.g., something has been moved, a book is open on the table, someone is in the room, or an artifact is missing).

Research Phone Calls

Ask players to look for recent messages on a phone and listen to each to uncover important information. They could also look at a call log of numbers to find out who the suspect was calling when or to try to figure out the most likely suspect by the frequency of calls.

Examine a Video Feed

Have your players tap into a video feed. This can be a pre-recorded pretend security footage video. Your players can gain access to it at some point during the game, and you can set it up to make it look like a live feed. Your players need to watch for the disappearance of an important item or the arrival of a key suspect.

Contact Others

Have your players communicate with someone on the outside, like the tech guy sitting in the van down the street. The tech guy can be imaginary, and your players can communicate with him through you. Pretend to have a tiny microphone in your ear you can hear him with.

For a more believable experience, get a friend to actually play the role of the tech guy and stay outside the room, ready to receive and exchange information. Your players could communicate with him through email, over the phone, or even with a walkie-talkie.

17

Techniques

Here are some overall techniques to guide you as you create the clues and puzzles in your escape room.

One Clue, One Use

A practice many commercial escape room facilities use is a "one clue, one use" rule. It means that each clue in an escape room will be used only once. It makes it a little easier on the players because once they use a clue for a piece of information, they can set it aside and focus on the remaining clues to solve the remaining tasks.

If you are breaking the "one clue, one use" rule, I would warn your players at the beginning. It does increase the difficulty of the room because players won't be able to use process of elimination to remove some clues and it will be harder to discern which clue(s) to use for each step of the game.

Breaking the "one clue, one use" rule can be done artfully, if a host is careful. At the end of the movie *National Treasure*, Ben Gates uses a pipe to open the treasure room. The pipe was a clue they found early in the movie and it had already served a purpose, but discovering a new, secret use at the end of the movie was kind of a fun twist. If you do something like this in your escape room, players might feel extra clever for discovering the second use (even if it's fairly obvious).

Split Up Information

One basic escape room technique is to divide up useful information in separate parts of the room. For example, players might need to identify a character in the game in order to deduce a computer password from the character's favorite pet. First players might need to look at a photo of the character that identifies the character's occupation but not name. Players then need to find a company photo directory to learn the character's name. A third clue, like a photo of a pet signed by the character, could finally reveal the password. This can be a way to stretch out puzzles to make them longer and require more pieces.

This puzzle has been broken into several steps. First players find the colored cards with the shapes of the states. Then they use the atlas to identify the state based on its shape. Finally, they use other pages in the atlas to figure out the state's capital so they can fill in the crossword.

Take the crossword puzzle from chapter eleven, for example. In it, players are given the names of states and must fill in the states' capital cities to complete the crossword. To add another layer to the puzzle, instead of listing the name of the state, we could display a picture of the state. It's one more step players have to take to solve the puzzle.

Arbitrary Puzzles

The less arbitrary you can make the puzzles in a room, the better. (*Arbitrary* in this case means puzzles that exist or work only because you say so and not because of logic or evidence or tying them into the plot.) If you are using a lot of host feedback puzzles, you can make them seem less arbitrary by working them into the narrative or creating clear visual reminders or reasons the puzzles work the way they do.

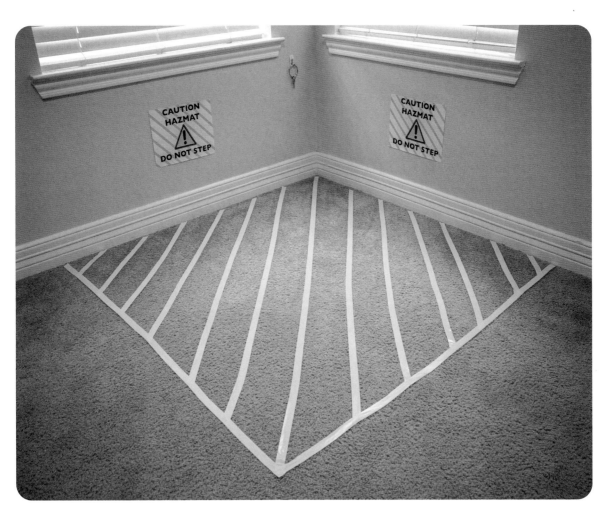

The section of floor players aren't allowed to step on is marked very clearly, making it obvious they need to find a creative way to reach the key (which you can see in the top center section of the photo).

TIP:

Try to work rules (like don't touch the decorations on the walls) into the narrative. If you are creating rules like limiting players from stepping on certain parts of the floor, try to create visual reminders for them (like lines created with tape) to help them with their suspension of disbelief. Try not to have clues or puzzles that work that way just because you say so.

Puzzles with Multiple Answer Choices

Many puzzles would lend themselves well to a multiple choice scenario. For example, a fun task for players to do would be to pour vinegar into a test tube of baking soda and watch for the chemical reaction that follows. To create a reason for them to do this, you could provide four test tubes, three with powdered sugar at the bottom and one with baking soda. Your players must figure out which is which by pouring the vinegar. You will of course want this activity to communicate some important information to your players, like a lock combination. You could label the test tubes—write the correct combination on the baking soda one and incorrect combinations on the other three. However, if you're providing a combination for a lock, only four choices really isn't that much. If your players wanted to skip the vinegar pouring entirely, they could just guess and check the four combinations until they get the right one.

If you do want to incorporate multiple choice like this, you can incorporate lots of options, too many to guess and check—like a paper list of fifty possible lock combinations. Since this isn't feasible with test tubes of baking soda, another option is to have several multiple-choice problems as part of one puzzle. For example, if you have a three-digit combination lock, make each number the correct answer to a separate multiple choice puzzle. Players can still guess and check for individual numbers of the combination, but if there are now three digits, each with four options, it becomes much more cumbersome to guess the whole combination.

Another way to work multiple choice into your escape room is to make it the last challenge where failure is a very real option, like cutting wires on an electronic panel. If players cut the wrong wire, security is alerted, and they lose. If you choose this strategy, make sure players know what's at stake, and make sure they have all the information they need to make the correct decision.

Alternate Solutions

Especially if you're dealing with physical objects, there might be multiple ways to solve a puzzle. For example, if you want your players to fish out a key with a magnet, they might instead find some tape and a stick in the room that they use. This could be fine, but it is possible that there's an alternate solution to a puzzle that would make solving the room much easier than you intend it to be.

For example, maybe you created an elaborate code that lets players decipher the words that are blacked out with marker in a typed letter. However, during the game, your players discover they can simply hold the paper to the light to read the blacked-out words. This is resourceful on their part, but if you spent hours making a custom code, you probably won't be very fulfilled to watch your players bypass it in seconds.

In situations like these, when you're creating and testing your room, make sure there are no alternate solutions to puzzles you want your players to solve in a certain way.

In the case of the blacked-out words, you could not type the words at all when you're creating your clue to make sure your players wouldn't be able to read them.

It is possible that you want alternate solutions to puzzles or are okay with them. Perhaps you provide two ways to solve a puzzle on purpose, one faster and one slightly more time consuming, and see which one your players figure out. For example, if players need batteries to put in a black light, you could lock a pair of batteries in a clear maze puzzle where players can see them. Players will see the batteries, realize they need them for the black light, and focus on opening the maze. An observant player, however, might notice the wall clock ticking on the wall and realize they can remove and use the batteries from that.

Outside Knowledge

Most escape rooms do not rely on players' outside knowledge. If something is needed to solve a clue or puzzle, like Morse code, the Morse code key should be somewhere in the room. Don't assume players know things that they may not.

The most common technique for escape rooms is to include the information (like a Morse code key) in the room. That way you know your players will have the information they need. This is often a better technique than letting your players use the internet to search for answers, which can take players out of the experience and distract them. Also, with a key you can control the information, whereas the information on the internet could be factually inconsistent with your puzzle.

TIP:
If there is specialized knowledge you *know* your players have, by all means, use it! Perhaps you're hosting an escape room for your colleagues in the linguistics department. You could absolutely code something with morphemes or Latin root words. If you're working with mathematicians, use more difficult math problems and terms. Using specialized knowledge that you know your players have can make them feel extra smart; not just *anyone* could have escaped that room, but they did! They're more than clever or just good at teamwork; they're skilled.

As Self-Guided as Possible

Try to use puzzles, codes, and ciphers that players can complete mostly on their own. It can be frustrating for players to have to read through (or listen to) lengthy instructions to solve something. If you do include a difficult type of puzzle or code that players have never done before, consider making them familiar with it before the game starts.

Additionally, you should avoid *offering* too much instruction. Even if you as a host have written yourself a role in the room, your goal should be to let your players do as much as they can with as little help from you as possible. Of course, you will end up giving them hints, but try to make your goal having your players do everything on their own.

Your Own Skills

Your DIY escape room will be catered to your players—and to you. Everyone has specialized skills, knowledge, or hobbies. Use those in your escape room to create unique puzzles and challenges. Your skill might be graphic design, so your room incorporates lots of custom images. Perhaps you're skilled at woodworking. In that case, make a custom box with a lock. Maybe you're an electrician and you can rig a puzzle that involves lights, switches, or electronics. If you're a science teacher, I bet you could come up with a neat puzzle using a microscope. If you're a crafter, you could make all sorts of fun props and puzzles. Maybe you could even hide a clue in a DIY bath bomb. If you're a baker, make a homemade fortune cookie with a clue inside. Use the technology, items, and know-how that's specific to you to make your room a success!

Conclusion

Now you have everything you need to create a stellar DIY escape room! You know how to create a story and how to structure the puzzles and clues. You have hundreds of ideas for different puzzles and challenges. You have tips and tricks on decorating, setup, and hosting. Hopefully this book has made you see that creating your own escape room is something that you can do, even if the task seemed daunting. Remember that as you create a room, you will go through drafts and changes, especially as you test your puzzles and clues in advance. The rewarding experience of watching friends or family play through a game you yourself created is worth it!

Acknowledgments

My biggest thank-you goes to my husband Josh, without whom there would be no book. Thank you for encouraging me, taking all the pictures, and testing all the ideas. Thank you for your opinions, advice, and patience. Thank you for the many date nights we spent doing research or shopping for supplies instead of doing fun stuff like seeing movies or going to dinner—but of course with you, it's all fun anyway.

A huge thank-you to everyone at Skyhorse who worked on the manuscript and design!

Thank you Carson and Annelise for thinking your mom's escape room stuff is cool and trying out new puzzles and ideas with me (and for being photography models). Thank you Grace for giving me time to write and letting me completely transform your bedroom for a little bit.

Thank you to my family for being so supportive, especially to my mom for all of her babysitting and photography help and to my sister Brenn for reading through my manuscript.

Thank you beautiful Wong family for your nice modeling work. You were perfect!

Thank you to all of my game testers over the years, you guinea pigs who were willing to try my brand-new rooms. Family/in-laws—brothers and sisters and parents—thanks for putting up with all of my escape room activities and requests at our family reunions. Friends—all of you who've come over to our house so I could pretend to lock you in a room—you've been so very helpful. Thank you also to Mom and Dad and your young single adults of the Armand Bayou branch for providing the largest group of testers I could ask for. You guys are awesome.

And really just a huge thank-you to anyone who's played any of my games, ever. It wouldn't be any fun without you!

Appendix

ASCII	
A	65
B	66
C	67
D	68
E	69
F	70
G	71
H	72
I	73
J	74
K	75
L	76
M	77
N	78
O	79
P	80
Q	81
R	82
S	83
T	84
U	85
V	86
W	87
X	88
Y	89
Z	90
0	48
1	49
2	50
3	51
4	52
5	53
6	54
7	55
8	56
9	57

Binary	
0	0000 0000
1	0000 0001
2	0000 0010
3	0000 0011
4	0000 0100
5	0000 0101
6	0000 0110
7	0000 0111
8	0000 1000
9	0000 1001
10	0000 1010
11	0000 1011
12	0000 1100
13	0000 1101
14	0000 1110
15	0000 1111
16	0001 0000
17	0001 0001
18	0001 0010
19	0001 0011
20	0001 0100
21	0001 0101
22	0001 0110
23	0001 0111
24	0001 1000
25	0001 1001
26	0001 1010
27	0001 1011
28	0001 1100
29	0001 1101
30	0001 1110
31	0001 1111
32	0010 0000

Braille

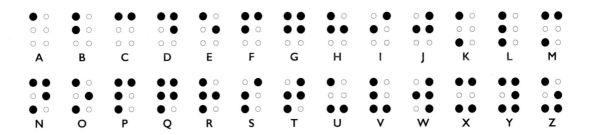

Letters That Reflect Well

Letters That Reflect Vertically

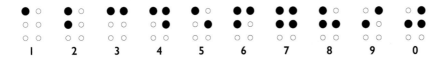

HAnnAH	HAnnAH
soup	quoz
slim	Milz
MondAY	YAbnoM
TsunAMi	iMAnuzT
snowMAn	nAMwonz

Letters That Reflect Horizontally

B C D E H I K O X I

BlOCKED	BlOCKED
CODEX	CODEX
COID	COID
ECHO	ECHO
ICEBOX	ICEBOX
ICE	ICE
lOCKED	lOCKED

Morse Code

A	•—		T	—
B	—•••		U	••—
C	—•—•		V	•••—
D	—••		W	•——
E	•		X	—••—
F	••—•		Y	—•——
G	——•		Z	——••
H	••••			
I	••			
J	•———		1	•————
K	—•—		2	••———
L	•—••		3	•••——
M	——		4	••••—
N	—•		5	•••••
O	———		6	—••••
P	•——•		7	——•••
Q	——•—		8	———••
R	•—•		9	————•
S	•••		0	—————

Pigpen

A	B	C		J	K	L
D	E	F		M	N	O
G	H	I		P	Q	R

S
T U
V

W
X Y
Z

A	B	C	D	E	F	G	H	I	J	K	L	M

N	O	P	Q	R	S	T	U	V	W	X	Y	Z

NATO Phonetic Alphabet

A	Alfa
B	Bravo
C	Charlie
D	Delta
E	Echo
F	Foxtrot
G	Golf
H	Hotel
I	India
J	Juliett
K	Kilo
L	Lima
M	Mike
N	November
O	Oscar
P	Papa
Q	Quebec
R	Romeo
S	Sierra
T	Tango
U	Uniform
V	Victor
W	Whiskey
X	X-ray
Y	Yankee
Z	Zulu

Roman Numerals

Arabic	Roman
1	I
2	II
3	III
4	IV
5	V
6	VI
7	VII
8	VIII
9	IX
10	X
11	XI
12	XII
13	XIII
14	XIV
15	XV
16	XVI
17	XVII
18	XVIII
19	XIX
20	XX
21	XXI
22	XXII
23	XXIII
24	XXIV
30	XXX
40	XL
50	L
60	LX
70	LXX
80	LXXX
90	XC
100	C

SEEK AND FIND

See page 99 for the solution.

Escape Room Clue Locations

Clue	Where It's Hidden

Bibliography

Brown, Dan. *The Da Vinci Code*. New York: Doubleday, 2003. Page 198.

Ciovacco, Justine, Kathleen A. Feeley, and Kristen Behrens. *State-by-State Atlas*. New York: DK Publishing, 2003.

Encyclopædia Britannica Online, s.v. "Code (communications)," https://www.britannica .com/topic/code-communications (accessed February 11, 2020).

Geek & Sundry. "Escape! With Janet Varney" (YouTube series). youtube.com/playlist? list=PL7atuZxmT957_N4O2Jp3bMXmq_Y7J-mK- (accessed February 11, 2020).

Magic Eye Inc. "FAQ." https://www.magiceye.com/faq/.

Magic Eye Inc. *Magic Eye Gallery: A Showing of 88 Images*. Kansas City: Andrews McMeel Publishing, 1995.

Media, Joey. "7 Steps for Writing Escape Room Narratives (And How to Find Opportunities to Write Them)." Stage 32, www.stage32.com/blog/7-Steps-for-Writing-Escape-Room -Narratives-And-How-to-Find-Opportunities-to-Write-Them.

Merriam-Webster's Collegiate Dictionary. 11th ed. Springfield, MA: Merriam-Webster, 2003. Also available at http://www.merriam-webster.com/.

Nicholson, Scott. "The State of Escape: Escape Room Design and Facilities." Paper presented at *Meaningful Play 2016*. Lansing, Michigan. scottnicholson.com/pubs/stateofescape .pdf.

Sargent, Epes. *Songs of the Sea, with Other Poems*. Boston: James Monroe, 1847. https://rpo .library.utoronto.ca/poems/life-ocean-wave.

Index

Link to Bonus Step-by-Step Escape Room!

Link: www.thediyescaperoombook.com/free-escape-room

Password: misty-aquacade-tightrope-gold